A PINK MIST

11/14/13

Judy,
Read this and you'll see that Jim really was the hero he has always claimed to be. :)

A PINK MIST

JOHN A. BERCAW

Creekside Press
Florence, Kentucky

ISBN 13: *9781482772807*

ISBN 10: 1482772809

Library of Congress Control Number: *2013905399*
CreateSpace Independent Publishing Platform
North Charleston, South Carolina

Map of South Vietnam

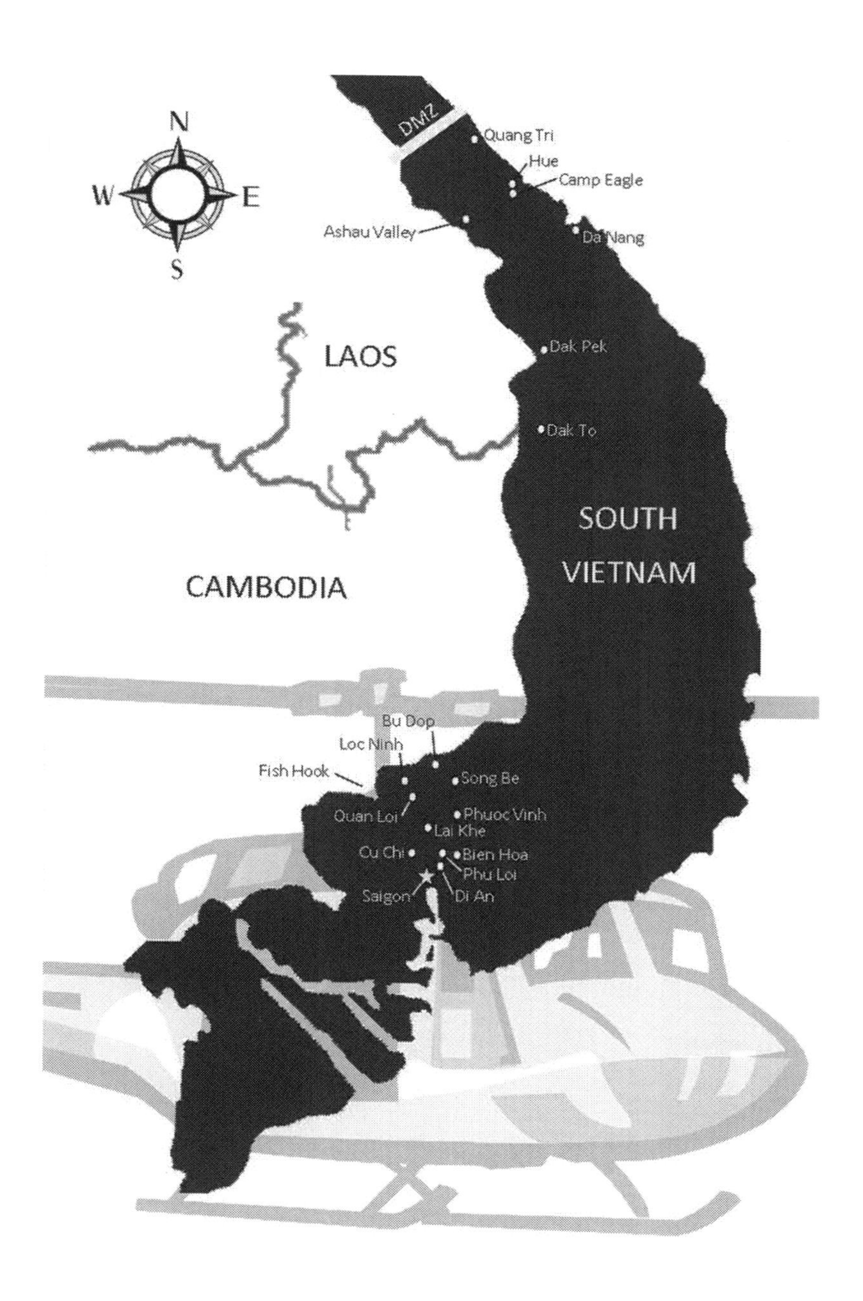

Bell UH-1H – Huey

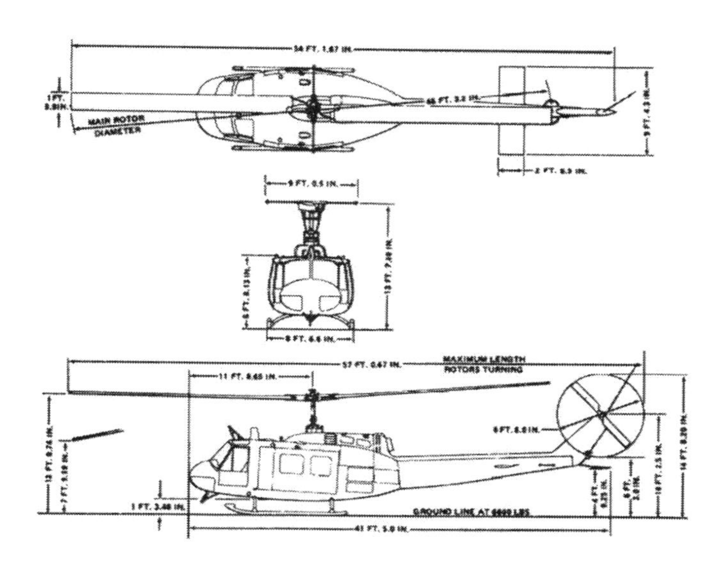

Bell OH-13S – Sioux

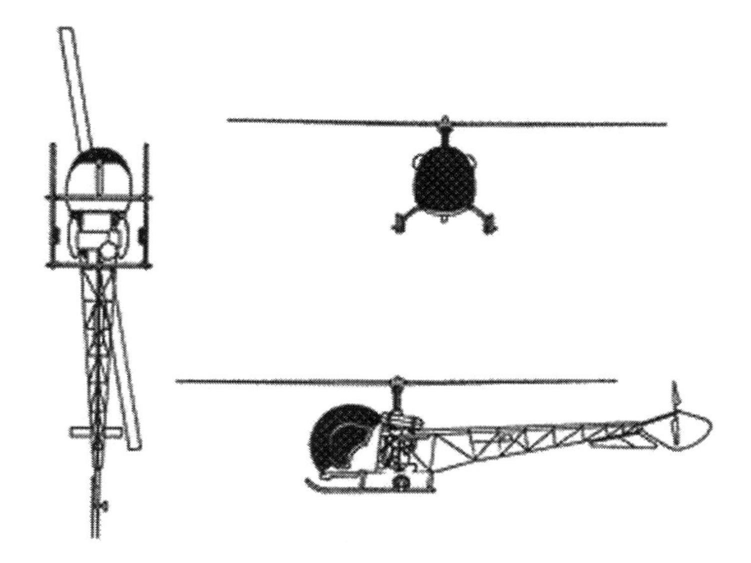

Dedication

Many people deserve to be included in this dedication, but I have decided on two men who instilled in me the discipline and the confidence necessary to survive in the military, combat, and life.

Marine Corps boot camp was a shock. At seventeen years old, I was an undisciplined and troubled high school dropout. The two men who greeted my fellow recruits and me were unlike any I had previously known. Highly disciplined, impeccably groomed to military standards, tough, fair, seemingly unafraid, and never demanding anything of us they could not do themselves, they impressed me as no one had. My memory of them continues to impress me to this day. The impact that they had on my life has been profound.

Their fates are unknown to me, but I sincerely hope they survived whatever the future had in store for them and they are now enjoying well-deserved retirements on some sunny shores. If they have not survived, I trust they have indeed found that the streets of Heaven are guarded by United States Marines.

It is with great respect and a large debt of gratitude that I dedicate this book to these two men.

- **Staff Sergeant W. M. Wolfe,** Platoon Commander, Third Battalion, Platoon 395, Marine Corps Recruit Depot, San Diego, California. October, 1960 – January, 1961

- **Corporal L. Kirkland,** Junior Drill Instructor, Third Battalion, Platoon 395, Marine Corps Recruit Depot, San Diego, California. October, 1960—January, 1961

Acknowledgments

- Cynthia Rupprecht Bercaw, my lovely wife, has tolerated my nonsense on many levels beyond any reasonable expectation. She served as my immediate editor and sounding board throughout the gestation period of this book.
- Frank Belsky, Jim Morgan, and Milo Overstreet: I shared the experience of combat and formed lifelong friendships with these men. Each of them assisted me with long-forgotten details and fading memories during the construction of this book.
- In addition, I wish to acknowledge the assistance and friendship of Al Fritz, Chuck Hagan, Howard Klein, Brian Wold and JJ Mateer. I found them via the Internet—or, perhaps, they found me.
- Susan Field, my first creative writing instructor, encouraged me and convinced me to change my focus to broaden my target audience.
- Wendy Chorot, my first professional editor, had an abundant supply of kind words and patience. She served as a teacher as much as an editor.
- Joseph Michael, a former infantry medic who answered some of my initial questions regarding Dustoff 46. He

introduced me to Michael Ballinger, a flight medic and the son of Major Ballinger, the pilot of Dustoff 46.

- Curt Bessette provided the renderings of the South Vietnam map and the Creekside Press logo in response to my last-minute request. In addition, he designed the bookmarks and the business cards I use as advertising handouts for this book.
- Neal Thompson assisted in the final preparation of my manuscript and helped guide me through the publishing maze. Neal flew Cobra helicopters in Vietnam in 1971-72, and he is the author of *RECKONING: Vietnam and America's Cold War Experience, 1945-1991* (See *Internet and Other Information*).
- I am deeply indebted to Diana Hacker and her wonderful guide to writing: Hacker, Diana, *A Writer's Reference, Sixth Edition,* Boston, Massachusetts, Bedford/St. Martin's, 2007, ISBN: 13: 978-0-312-45025-0
- The Internet: without this marvelous tool, my research for this book would have been long and difficult. I used many websites dedicated in one way or another to providing information about Vietnam and other sites that provided writing assistance. I do not think I can overstate the benefits of the speed and ease of email and the ability to find people with whom I worked so long ago. The following are some sites that I used extensively:

    - Dictionary.com:
      http://dictionary.reference.com/
    - Thesaurus.com:
      http://thesaurus.reference.com/

- Quoteland.com:
  http://www.quoteland.com/
- Ray's Map Room:
  http://www.rjsmith.com/topo_map.html
- Vietnam Helicopter Pilots Association:
  http://www.vhpa.org
- Wikipedia:
  http://en.wikipedia.org/wiki/Main_Page
- Google Earth

Preface

We do not remember days; we remember moments.

~CESARE PAVESE

My troubled years as a teenager prompted me to join the Marine Corps in late 1960. After the Marines, I moved to Chicago to attend school and try to decide what I wanted to do with my life. The Vietnam War and a call from the Army for helicopter pilots, along with my growing dissatisfaction with what I was doing, encouraged me to reenter the military to fulfill my long-held dream of becoming a pilot. This memoir[1] is an account of some of these events and the year I spent in Vietnam. Each chapter can stand alone—as do each of my memories.

This memoir is as accurate as I could make it. However, while conducting the necessary research and communicating with old comrades, I came to the inescapable conclusion that some of my memories were faulty. In a couple of instances, I have combined events to provide a more interesting reading experience. The beginning of the chapter entitled "Turning Point" deviates from the truth ever so slightly. To do otherwise would have required providing a significant amount

1 "Memoirs means when you put down the good things you ought to have done and leave out the bad ones you did do." ~Will Rogers, enotes.com Website, 2012 < http://www.enotes.com/topic/Memoir >

of setup information that would have distracted from the actual story. It is close enough to the truth, and the events of the rest of the chapter are as precise as I can remember them. I re-created conversations based on my best memories, and in some instances based on realistic expectations for the situations. Unit call signs are my invention. Aircraft call signs are reasonably accurate. I have provided pronunciation assistance for some of the place names throughout this book. However, the pronunciations are those used by American soldiers in Vietnam. They are not necessarily correct. In addition, my friend Jim Morgan has somewhat different memories of some of the adventures that we shared. We spent some quality time together, along with some good Kentucky bourbon, to revisit those memories and settle any differences.

I tried to write with humor when possible and with compassion, but a touch of bitterness and sarcasm crept in at times.

One of the things I came to appreciate while researching and writing this memoir is that most of the men I consider my friends have military backgrounds. Most of them are former pilots—usually helicopter pilots—and more likely than not they experienced firsthand what Justice Oliver Wendell Holmes, Jr. described as, "the incommunicable experience of war."

John A. Bercaw
Tuesday, April 9, 2013
Florence, Kentucky

We make fun of people, things, and ideas that threaten us. In doing so, we lessen the sense of threat.

~RICK WALTON

A joke popular with the student helicopter pilots of WORWAC class # 67–13

A lady is doing her housework one day when the doorbell rings. She opens the door and finds a man from Western Union standing outside.

"Oh, how wonderful," she says, "I've never had a singing telegram before."

"Sorry, ma'am," the man replies. "This is not a singing one."

"Oh, you must—you must," the lady begs. "Please open it, and sing it to me."

Reluctantly, he opens the telegram, takes a deep breath and breaks into song. "Your son was killed in Vietnam, doo-dah, doo-dah. Your son was killed in Vietnam, oh, doo-dah day."

Passing the Torch

There will come a time when you believe everything is finished. That will be the beginning.

~Louis L'Amour

Summer, 1969—Hunter Army Airfield, Savannah, Georgia

Facedown on the hot cement, I coughed from the dust that my heavy breathing had raised. After a moment of confusion as I wondered how I had gotten to that position, I remembered the explosion.

While walking across the ramp covered with parked TH-13T and Huey helicopters, I had been reviewing the training flights that I had just completed with my two students and thinking about how to tie it all in with the procedures we would cover the next day. I was tired. Remembering the time that I had spent learning to fly Army helicopters, I knew my students were exhausted.

Was it an explosion? Incoming? No. One of the helicopters had backfired. Yes. That was it—just a backfire. I glanced up to see both students looking down at me. The closest one looked back at the other and said, "Great. Is this what I can look forward to?"

Table of Contents

A PINK MIST

IN THE BEGINNING

1
A Portent

Every man has his own destiny; the only imperative is to follow it, to accept it, no matter where it leads him.

~HENRY MILLER

1950—Hulman Field, Terre Haute, Indiana

Fascinated I stared at the strange-looking aircraft parked near the flight operations building. It looked nothing like an airplane. It reminded me of a dragonfly. A large group of adults also vied to see the machine. They kept jostling me, and I had to struggle to stay in the front of the pack. It was the first helicopter that I, and most of the other watchers, had ever seen—the first military helicopter began churning up the skies just six years prior.[2]

2 In April 1944, Lt. Carter Harmon, flying an Army Sikorsky YR-4B helicopter, rescued four men—three of them wounded—during a two-day operation deep in the jungle behind Japanese lines. This operation took place fifteen miles west of Mawlu, Burma, now called Myanmar.

Eventually the pilot strode out of the operations building and over to the aircraft where he poked, prodded, and shook some parts and looked inside and under other parts. Then apparently satisfied that the helicopter was safe to fly he crawled inside and started the engine. With a bang and a roar, the helicopter thundered to life causing me to jump. At first, the rotor blades moved slowly, making swishing noises as they turned. Then the blades rapidly gathered speed until they were just a noisy blur. The protesting engine growled as the ungainly contraption rose about three feet off the ground. Hats sailed away and stinging dust brought tears to many an eye as the helicopter hovered for a moment before turning to its left. Dipping its nose, it crept forward a few feet and then rose into the air in defiance of gravity and logic. After flying a short distance away the pilot banked hard to the left and flew back over the crowd, thrilling everyone—especially me.

Fascinated with helicopters from that point forward I obtained a plastic Revell model of the Bell H-13 Sioux and built it with as much care as could be expected of a seven-year-old boy. Holding the model as the excess glue oozed out from between the pieces, I imagined myself swooping in under fire to rescue wounded soldiers. I would eventually fly this aircraft in another war—another decade. However, this was a secret hidden in the future.

2
Preflight

Hold fast to dreams, for if dreams die, life is a broken winged bird that cannot fly.

~Langston Hughes

Circa 1950—A farm just south of Vermilion, Illinois

Sitting about ten feet above the ground, I remained as motionless as a mountain lion waiting for prey to wander carelessly beneath me.

Climbing trees was my passion even though I did not know at the time what passion was or that I had one. Each tree presented a challenge, and I conquered every tree on the farm except for the big maples. They did not branch out until ten to twelve feet above the ground, and the trunks were too wide to shinny up.

Out of all of the trees I climbed only one remained my favorite: an apple tree that produced small green apples that

I ate even though they were hard and slightly bitter. This tree branched out about three feet above the ground making it easy for me to begin my climb. About ten feet up a convergence of branches created an area where I could sit—complete with a backrest and a footrest like a chair. Sometimes, I would sit there for nearly the entire day dreaming of being a hero, visiting faraway places and having nearby friends—other children with whom I could play.

As I was not heavy, and the tree was easy to climb, I could climb all the way to the top until my body from the waist up cleared the top of the tree. Feeling like a minor god, I could view almost the entire farm and spy on anyone in the area. It never occurred to the adults to look for me way up there sticking out the top of the tree like an errant limb. Free from the constraints and realities of life on the ground I spent a lot of time up in that tree.

3
Turning Point

Painful as it may be, a significant emotional event can be the catalyst for choosing a direction that serves us – and those around us – more effectively. Look for the learning.

~Louisa May Alcott

Summer, 1959—Vermilion, Illinois

Handcuffs hurt—hard metal clashed with tender wrist bones. For some reason I found this surprising as I sat in the back seat of a police car with my hands restrained behind me. The car seemed huge and I felt very small. A growing group of people stood around the car watching me and saying things like, "I always knew he'd end up like this." The humiliation factor kicked in, and I became intensely angry with myself for proving everyone right.

My grandfather had always told me that I would end up in jail by the time I was sixteen, and guess what—there I was, just sixteen and on my way to jail. I hoped that everyone was happy with this turn of events. I felt that this was probably the first time in my life that I had not disappointed someone.

"John, is that understood?"

The sheriff was talking, and I realized I had not heard a word. I just grunted and kept my head down. How had I gotten myself into this mess?

Just a short time before, I had been with my girlfriend. She was being very friendly, and I was pretty sure I was going to get lucky. Unfortunately, someone started pounding on the door. I tried to ignore it, but it continued without letting up. I opened the door, and my buddy told me to come down to the corner because so-and-so was bad-mouthing us. Like a fool I left the comfort of an affectionate girlfriend to go and see so-and-so. As soon as my friend and I reached the corner, everyone started yelling, shoving, and punching one another. Tires crunched on the gravel on the side of the road. It was the sheriff. He stepped out of his car and the fighting quickly ceased. All the time I just wanted to go back to my girlfriend.

So-and-so was talking to the sheriff and calling him by name. The sheriff was asking him how his mother was doing. Then so-and-so was going home, and I was going to jail. *Shit.*

The left cuff was too tight, and my hand had gone numb. The sheriff told me I would be okay until we got to the jail.

While riding in the car and walking into the jail, I kept my head down hoping that no one would see me. Processing into the jail was a blur, and I numbly went wherever anyone directed. In a very short time, I found myself in a jail cell. It looked nothing like those that I had seen in western TV shows like *Gunsmoke*. The cellblock sat in the middle of a large room. All sides were about ten feet away from the outer walls and the barred windows. The flatiron bars of the cells crisscrossed creating little one-inch-by-one-inch holes that required me to close one eye to see outside of the cell. Four cells shared one toilet, which was located in the middle of what was essentially a fifth cell. The toilet lacked any privacy. The single door to the cellblock opened only after the doors to each cell locked. Each cell contained four bunk beds—two per side. The aisle between them was about as wide as my shoulders. It took just three steps to walk from the door to the opposite side, where food trays arrived through a small rectangular opening. The food offered on the first day looked terrible. Still in my punk mode, I refused to eat—my second mistake of the day. Starving when I arrived I never felt sated during my incarceration.

A loud-mouthed prick in the next cell gave me a hard time because I was the new guy. I gave it right back, but it relieved me that a cell separated us. I did not want to be there. I did not feel tough, and I certainly did not want to be around that asshole.

Lying on my bunk and looking at the hard, gray, and very limited world I now inhabited, I began to feel sorry for myself. I was sixteen years old for Chrissake, and I did not belong here. Okay, so I'd had a couple of fights, and I had stolen some stuff—mostly gasoline siphoned out of cars so that my buddies and I could ride around the back roads in the middle of the night after we had all sneaked out of our homes. It was true that I'd gotten drunk and ridden my motorcycle like a maniac, but even I realized that I was lucky not to have foolishly killed myself. Beginning my sophomore year, cutting school at least once or twice a week became a routine. In addition, it seemed that all fathers had warned their daughters about me. It amused me that the warnings sometimes backfired. More than one girl had made it known to me that she was interested specifically because of my bad-boy image. However, much of that reputation was just talk. Mostly I was scared and full of self-doubt.

The sheriff told me that he had called my parents, but no one came. It was obvious that I was going to spend the whole damn night in that goddamned jail with a bunch of scary people. *Shit.*

Sometime during the night, the loud-mouthed prick began yelling at another prisoner, and soon everyone was yelling, swearing, and threatening one another between the cells. Most of the time, I could not even identify those doing the yelling. Then the sheriff came in and took the asshole out to spend the night with the "big boys." I did not even know there was a big-boy section in the building. I thought I was in the main jail. After that, I decided that the section I was in must be for the little boys—like me.

Breakfast came early and I scarfed it down. The meals turned out to be the highlights of the day. Otherwise, the prisoners just sat in their cells contemplating their future. Pacing back and forth passed some time, but mostly I lay on my bunk wallowing in self-pity.

On the second evening my parents came. My dad told me how things were going to change and how the two of us were going to spend time doing things together. I embarrassed myself by crying. My mother never said a word.

The next day, the sheriff came and let me out of the cell-block. I sat on the broad sill of one of the barred windows watching the cars and people on the street below and wondering how the world would receive me when I got out.

On the third day my father's female friend came to take me home. I was light-headed and had difficulty walking because I was hungry, and I had been lying on my bunk for almost three days. I found that my troublemaker reputation had grown, but I no longer wanted it.

I would remember very little about my trial. I stood in front of the judge, staring out a window wanting to be elsewhere. The prosecutor seemed very angry, and he argued vehemently for the judge to give me a six-month sentence in the county jail. I could not understand what I had done to make him so angry. I didn't even know the man. I ended up receiving indefinite probation. When I turned seventeen, I quit high school and joined the Marines.

4
A New Beginning

I cannot say whether things will get better if we change; what I can say is they must change if they are to get better.

~GEORG CHRISTOPH LICHTENBERG

Sunday, October 9, 1960—Vermilion, Illinois

Rising early, I dressed in my best clothes: white shirt, black slacks, black sport coat, black socks, and black penny loafers. Feeling much older than my seventeen years, I questioned my future as images of the past swirled through my head. I found courage in the realization that I must accept the new direction my life had taken. I saw all other options as closed, unappealing, or just plain wrong. My goodbyes with my family were muted and short. Later that morning my friend John Hurst picked me up, and we headed over to the drag strip in Terre Haute, Indiana to watch the races.

Late in the afternoon, one of the dragsters blew an engine and oil shot out of the exhaust stacks, arching high in the air before dropping onto the audience and depositing black oil stains on my shirt. It somehow seemed fitting that I would leave home with a soiled shirt.

After watching the races and eating an uninspired meal at the local hamburger joint, nearly deserted and depressing on a Sunday evening, Hurst dropped me off at the Greyhound bus station. Surrendering my ticket, which the Marine Corps had provided, I found myself to be the only passenger on the bus to Indianapolis. Riding through the evening gloom, I felt totally disconnected from my past, while missing a life that was never mine. Thus began the most important transition of my life.

UNITED STATES MARINE CORPS

5
Semper Fidelis

Recognition is the greatest motivator.

~Gerard C. Eakedale

October 12, 1960—Marine Corps Recruit Depot, San Diego, California

"Move, move, move!"

These commands resulted in a confusion of flailing arms and legs along with more than a few bumps and curses in the scramble to get out of the canvas-covered pickup truck. A few men struggled with suitcases. I had no suitcase, as my recruiter had advised me to take nothing more than what I would be wearing. Once off the truck some of the men moved quickly to the designated spot. Some just walked. This irritated the Marine sergeant.

"Move!" The word snapped through the calm San Diego air and caused all of us to jump and hustle. "No one told you to walk."

With a minimum of pushing, shoving, and cursing, we eventually managed to assemble ourselves as instructed, standing with our feet positioned on top of yellow footprints painted on the cement. The sergeant, impressive in his Dress Blue uniform, strolled back and forth as he glared at us.

"I am happy you ladies could finally get with the program. Now when I tell you to move, you are going to go through the hatch in front of you, move rapidly down the passageway—do *not* run—turn right at the intersection, and go into the room at the end, where you will be issued your initial clothing. Is. That. Under. Stood?"

A few of the recruits mumbled, "Yes." One or two of them said, "Yes, sir."

"From now on when anyone gives you an order, you will respond smartly with, 'Yes, sir.' Is that understood?"

"Yes, sir."

"I can't hear you people."

"Yes, sir." It was a little louder this time.

"What? I still can't hear you."

"Yes, sir!"

"Better. Better. Now move, move, move."

A rush for the hatch resulted in a lot of pushing and shoving to get through. Having already forgotten the orders I hung back just a bit so that I could follow someone who I hoped would remember the sergeant's instructions. Once we made it through the door, a long corridor greeted us. The floor glistened from endless waxing and buffing by new recruits. Several Marines stood at varying intervals along the hallway waiting for us. One of the men with a suitcase stumbled and fell.

"Out-*fucking*-standing, maggot. I told you people to walk. What part of those instructions do you not understand?"

The sergeant screamed now, and just like one dog barking causes every other dog in the area to start barking, the other Marines stationed along the hallway joined in until only screaming and confusion reigned. The passageway was a gauntlet of tough-looking Marines armed with loud harsh words. Struggling to look like I was walking as I raced down the hallway, I felt the first flicker of doubt about my decision to join the Marines.

"Move it, people. My grandmother moves faster than you, and she's dead."

As I turned right at the intersection, I collided with several others who had paused at the entrance to the room. This resulted in another bout of pushing and shoving. In anger and frustration, men were elbowing each other and someone's stupid suitcase painfully hit my left shin. Everyone was cursing.

"Quiet!" The word ricocheted off the walls. "No one gave you permission to talk."

Reaching the end of the passageway, I entered a room that contained more screaming Marines. Someone thrust a dented galvanized bucket into my hand and directed me to the right behind the men who had entered the room ahead of me.

"Place your bucket in front of you and kneel down behind it," someone inside the room instructed us as we entered.

I did this.

"Kneel, numbnuts. No one told you to sit."

My body jerked involuntarily at this command. After determining that I was in fact kneeling and not sitting, I discretely glanced around, trying to determine the identity of numbnuts.

People began to fling things at me: green pants; a yellow sweatshirt emblazoned in red on the front with "United States Marine Corps" and the Eagle, Globe, and Anchor logo; a white laundry bag; and green wool socks. A man standing in the front of the room pointed directly at me demanding to know my shoe size. When I hesitated, he said that I looked like a nine-and-a-half, and he threw some gym shoes in my direction. Additional items headed my way: a green cap that was somewhat reminiscent of a railroad engineer's hat, a tan belt, a brass belt buckle, white T-shirts, white boxer shorts with very high waistbands, a nasty-looking bar of soap called Fels-Naptha, a small notepad, and a mechanical pencil. After we received all of the items and placed them dutifully in our buckets, we moved out of the room, down a passageway, up some stairs, and into a room filled with military bunk beds.

Everyone began to talk, asking questions about what we were supposed to do and where we were supposed to go. Then everyone got quiet—except for me. Oblivious, I continued asking another bewildered recruit questions. After a moment, I became aware of the complete silence in the room, and then I sensed a presence standing very close to me. Turning I found myself face-to-face with a scowling man who was a touch taller than I was. He was wearing green trousers; a tan shirt; a tan tie; a gold tie clasp decorated with a tiny Eagle, Globe, and Anchor; a Smokey Bear hat; and a nametag engraved with the name *Kirkland*. Confidence and power radiated from him like light from a lantern. His dark eyes, no more than ten inches away, locked onto mine.

"What's your name, maggot?"

His low tone, in contrast to the constant yelling we had endured thus far startled me.

"John Bercaw."

"Your name is 'Private Bercaw, sir.' Is that understood?"

"Yes."

"What?" It was more of a snapping sound than a word.

"Yes, sir," I said. "My name is Private Bercaw, sir."

"Are we inconveniencing you, Private Bercaw?"

"Uh, no, sir."

"Are you sure, Private Bercaw?"

"No, sir. I mean, yes, sir."

"Do you want your mama, Private Bercaw?"

"No, sir."

"Are you looking for sympathy, Private Bercaw?"

"Uh, no, sir."

"Are you sure, Private Bercaw? You sound a little confused."

"No, sir."

"No? You're not sure?"

"I mean yes, sir, I'm sure." This was worse than standing in front of the blackboard in school, chalk in hand, with no idea what to write.

"Well if you need any sympathy while you are here, and that may not be very long, Private Bercaw," he said, drawing out the word "long," "you'll find it in the dictionary. It's somewhere between *shit* and *syphilis*."

"Uh, yes, sir," I said, now nearly overcome with an irrational desire to laugh.

"Do you find me funny, Private Bercaw?"

"Uh, no, sir," I said, struggling to maintain my composure. I could feel my face turning red.

"Do you think you can get with the program and join the rest of your platoon, Private Bercaw?"

"Yes, sir."

"I've got my eye on you. Fuck up and I'll be all over you like stink on shit. Is that understood, Private Bercaw?"

"Yes, sir!"

6
Discipline

From the first day of recruit training, discipline is fostered in every Marine.

~UNITED STATES MARINE CORPS WEBSITE, 2008 <HTTP://WWW.MARINES.COM>

Late 1960—Marine Corps Recruit Depot, San Diego, California

"Forward. March."

It did not sound like he said "march." It came out sounding like "huh." It was more like the crack of a whip, an explosion of sound unique to each drill instructor that they used to end every command on the parade field.

With my left foot perfectly synchronized with every other man in the platoon, I stepped forward to begin another long day as a Marine recruit.

Boot camp was all about discipline. Much to my surprise, we received little training involving tactics or equipment—with the exception of the M1 rifle. We were not taught how to fire various types of weaponry or how to maneuver in combat. They did not teach us any of the things that I had thought the Marines would teach me when I arrived at their gates, young, ignorant, pimply-faced, in poor physical shape, and undisciplined.

Instead, I discovered that boot camp was about changing, gaining physical and mental strength, developing and understanding the value of teamwork under stressful conditions, and starting to respect myself. We learned about Marine Corps history and organization, we learned the importance of obeying orders, and we were subjected to discipline, discipline, and still more discipline. Our drill instructors made us understand that if our hearts were still beating we had the strength to keep moving. We learned that upon finding ourselves in desperate situations with no ideas about what to do, it was better to do something—anything—than to do nothing. We memorized the Marine Corps Hymn.

All Marines are first and foremost riflemen, and each recruit and his rifle are inseparable. Always we carried them, cleaned them, disassembled them, and reassembled them. Then we did this blindfolded. Eventually we fired them. Sometimes we slept with them. We learned that the most important skill for a good Marine to possess is successful qualification on the rifle range. A Marine who failed to qualify was an unhappy Marine.

We marched everywhere. We marched in the dark before the sun came up. We marched to class, and we marched for punishment. We marched in the morning, and we marched in the afternoon. We practiced marching so that we could outperform the other platoons in our series. We marched and we carried our rifles. We marched until our feet became numb and our arms ached from carrying the nine-point-five-pound M1 Garand Rifles, which felt like fifty-pounds long before the day ended. We marched until the bottoms of our feet were flat, as if a carpenter had planed them. Marines march by listening to the sound of their heels striking the ground, and we marched until we had to have the heels replaced on both pairs of our issued boots. We marched to the mess hall for a frustratingly short three-times-a-day break. "Get in. Get ate. Get out," were the commands.

As we marched and listened to the never-ending commands, we looked straight ahead at the back of the head of the person directly in front of us. We did this until we could do it mindlessly, thinking of other things and places. We did this until we would almost forget how many hours remained before lights out and the blessed oblivion of a deep and dreamless sleep.

Sometimes, when not perfectly synchronized as our heels struck the blacktop, it sounded like *cl-clump, cl-clump, cl-clump*.

"Le'l, le'l, le'l, rye, le'l." The drill instructor worked to get us synchronized again.

But there were moments when we synchronized our movements to the degree that we seemed as one. *Clump, clump, clump*. The sound was hypnotic. Magnified exponentially, it became part of our souls. Eighty heels were but one. It was always there, even when our minds drifted off to girlfriends, other locales, and the luxury of not doing anything. When this happened, when the sound of but one heel struck the ground, it felt like power.

"Left shoulder," commanded the drill instructor. "Huh." One rifle moved.

"Column left. Huh." One individual turned.

Clump. One foot struck the ground. *Clump*. The other foot struck the ground. Power. We *were* invincible.

"Right shoulder. Huh."

Eventually, our rhythm would begin to fall apart resulting in the *cl-clump, cl-clump* sounds as we marched endlessly from one end of the mile-long parade field to the other. I always tried to bring it back, to make it continue through sheer willpower. Had I been successful, I could have marched forever.

UNITED STATES ARMY

7
First Flight

Oh! I have slipped the surly bonds of earth
And danced the skies on laughter-silvered wings…

~**RCAF Flight-Lieutenant John Gillespie Magee Jr.**

January, 1967—U.S. Army Primary Helicopter Flight Training Center, Fort Wolters, Texas

With my arms flailing, I searched for something solid to grab, even as I realized that anything reachable was plunging toward the earth at the same terrifying speed as I was. This small detail did not matter; I had to hold onto something.

Only moments before, my flight instructor Mr. Ragle had asked, "See the field with the lone tree in the middle?"

I looked down and saw fields and trees all the way to the horizon. "Yes, sir."

"I'm going to do an autorotation to the field, and then we'll practice some hovering. Ready?"

"Ready."

With that, Mr. Ragle rolled the throttle off. An ominous silence surrounded us as we began a sickening plunge toward what seemed like our certain deaths. Feeling like an egg that had just rolled over the edge of a table, I changed my mind; I was not ready. I was most certainly a vision of terror as we streaked toward the ground, and I probably screamed like a little girl. However, any such unmanly behavior lies buried forever in my subconscious memory.

Autorotation refers to the state that a helicopter enters if the engine fails—a state that allows for a single landing. I felt that the appropriate authorities should rename this maneuver to reflect its true nature: A Terrifying Death Plunge from the Sky to Some Godforsaken Cow Pasture in The-Middle-of-Nowhere, Texas.

Just as I was beginning to wonder if my life had flashed before my eyes and I had somehow missed it, Mr. Ragle rolled the power back on and leveled off about three feet above the ground in the previously unidentified—by me—field in front of the previously unidentified—again, by me—lone tree. This flight, scheduled to last an hour, had just begun, but I had already had enough.

During the previous month, I had read and reread the Army manual on how to fly a helicopter, and I felt confident that I could do it. *Make small adjustments to the controls,* it said, *and once made, do not make any additional adjustments unless necessary. Adjustment of any one control requires the corresponding adjustments of all of the other controls,* it said—or something like that. This sounded simple enough. The book explained each control: the pedals; the cyclic (the lever mounted on the floor and sticking up between your knees); the collective (the lever on your left); and the throttle. The latter was used to keep the engine RPM within the confines of the green arc that was painted on the instrument. Okay. So far I was good. The manual mentioned something called translational lift, but this was too much information for me at that moment.

Mr. Ragle pressed the intercom switch. "Get on the controls with me."

I did, and we hovered virtually motionless, three feet above the ground, facing the lonely tree. I could feel him making small adjustments to the controls, and it all seemed to coincide with the manual's instructions.

After a bit, he asked, "Are you ready?"

Foolishly, for the second time that day, I replied with, "Ready."

"You have the controls."

"I have the controls."

And that was the last I saw of the tree—or the ground. No. Wait. There was the ground—now the only thing I could see through the windshield. By the time I realized it was not desirable to have the ground in that position, it had disappeared again. I did not even know if I was still in the field, but I felt certain that I was still in Texas. It is, after all, a big state.

I felt Mr. Ragle's presence on the cyclic and the pedals.

He said, "I have the controls."

"You have the controls."

I had difficulty getting my hands to relax enough to let go. Pain shot through them as I uncurled each finger.

"This time just put your feet on the pedals. I'll handle the cyclic and the collective."

"Okay." That sounded simple enough. I placed my feet on the pedals.

"Are you ready?"

There was that damn word again.

"Ready."

He removed his feet from the pedals, and that stupid tree started moving to the right. I tried to work the pedals, but they were frozen. *Jeez, we have a malfunction of the flight controls*. This could not be good.

"Relax your legs."

"What?"

"Relax your legs."

How embarrassing. I had been pressing with both feet. However, when I relaxed my left leg my right leg shot straight out, and I watched in horror as the tree zoomed out of sight to the left. Now I needed to make another correction, but the stupid pedals had frozen again. Apparently, both of my legs, which were imitating toggle switches, only worked in one of two positions: fully bent at the knee or fully extended. Relaxing my right leg and pressing the left pedal with all of the skill and coordination of a stoned drunk I glimpsed the tree briefly as it zoomed from left to right and then out of sight again. This no longer mattered very much, as the sweat streaming into my eyes had nearly blinded me.

Mr. Ragle then had me try each of the other controls individually. None of the damn things worked the way that the manual indicated they would, and I was certain we had been flying long enough to run out of fuel. I wanted to hear the engine sputter and quit so that we could just sit and observe that elusive tree until someone came to pick us up. I wondered if Mr. Terry, my TAC Officer, would let me take a nap.

After an interminable period, Mr. Ragle took the controls. We climbed back to altitude, and I became terrified that he would do that death-plunge thing again. I would live in dread of this during my entire time in flight school. Later, as I gained experience the instructors tried to surprise me with these maneuvers. Once surprised they actually expected me to do something with the aircraft. One time I nearly landed on a flock of sheep. I had thought they would move out of the way, but the stupid animals just stood there looking up at me. Anyway, that is the direction we were headed in when the instructor rolled the throttle off. Who was I to question aerodynamics? Keeping the helicopter upright should gain me some sort of praise, right?

"You have the controls."

"I have the controls."

I sighed—a big, long, heavy sigh.

We flew along five hundred feet above the endless Texas terrain. Compared to the trauma near the ground this qualified as relaxing. I spent some time studying the instruments to see if I could make any sense of them, and I tried unsuccessfully to find the plunging-to-your-death indicator. I decided that the pilot made this assumption when all of the instruments displayed really scary things and you felt that sickening plunge like a trapdoor had just opened and you were waiting for the snap that comes upon reaching the end of your rope.

The instrumentation of our small helicopter included an airspeed indicator, an altimeter, a slip indicator (this one still confused me), and the previously mentioned engine RPM indicator. So that one does not become bored, helicopters have two needles associated with this device. One measures engine RPM, and the other represents the rotor RPM. Pilots are supposed to keep them joined, except when they are performing the death-plunge maneuver—a major problem at that point in my flying career. Actually, at that point in my flying career, everything was a problem.

We flew back through a bewildering series of radio calls, mysterious roadways in the sky, and a multitude of other helicopters. It reminded me of rush hour in Chicago only it was a lot more terrifying. On the ground, I looked down at my flight suit now soaked in sweat, and then I took my flight gloves off and saw the imprints of the control handles in the palms of my hands. Surely, my fledgling career had ended before it had the chance to begin.

"Tomorrow we will do pretty much the same as today," Mr. Ragle said. "Are you ready?"

"Ready."

In just one hour, I had come to hate this word. The meaning had changed. Henceforth, the result of hearing one of my instructors ask if I was ready, was an immediate adrenalin rush and a bad case of goose bumps, along with feelings of great foreboding.

Dazed I walked back to join the rest of my classmates. It relieved me somewhat to notice that the flight suits of all the students were soaked in sweat. I am guessing that Mr. Ragle and the other instructors went somewhere to have a drink and a good laugh.

8
Temporary Disorientation

Pilots never get lost; they are only temporarily disoriented.

~UNKNOWN

Early 1967—U. S. Army Primary Helicopter Flight Training Center, Fort Wolters, Texas

I was lost. How had this happened? Departing Possum Kingdom Lake, I had headed southeast expecting to eventually see the town of Mineral Wells and the fourteen-story Baker Hotel—the highest structure in that part of Texas. I then planned to head over to the Downing Army Heliport. Unfortunately, haze restricted visibility, and I had not been paying close attention to the map. Actually, I had not been paying *any* attention to the map, and I had gotten myself lost.

Spotting one of the many stage fields, I flew toward it, hoping to see the stage field's name on the roof of the tower. Unfortunately, I had stumbled onto a stage field with no name on the roof. *Crap*!

Departing, I tried to gain some altitude to see if I could spot the Baker Hotel, but the visibility dropped off rapidly as I climbed higher. I became afraid of losing sight of the ground, so I descended back to about five hundred feet. I needed a plan. Perhaps I could find another stage field.

I had no luck locating a stage field, but I did spot a road crew working beside a highway. I landed, swallowed my pride, exited the aircraft with my map, approached the crew, and asked for our location. Hooting, hollering, and pounding one another on the back, they refused to tell me their location. It seemed that I was the comic relief for the day. I wished I had a weapon—then we would have seen how damned funny it was.

I was officially late, but I still could not get myself to call and announce that I was lost. I wandered around for a while longer looking for anything that would identify my location. Eventually, my fuel gauge indicated that I should land while I still had power. Spotting a crossroads with a gas station and a big field in the back, I landed, shut down the engine, and made my way into the gas station. Borrowing the phone, I called the local Flight Service Station, gave them my location, and asked them to give this information to my flight commander along with a request for fuel.

After I finished, I went out front and sat on one of the steps.

A beefy salesman followed me out of the building and began to amuse himself at my expense. "Are you one of them Army helicopter students from up there at Fort Wolters?"

"Yes, I am."

"And you're lost?"

"Yes, I am."

"Boy, I bet you're in a heap o' trouble." He then let out a roar of good-old-boy laughter.

Silently I agreed with him, but I still wished I had a weapon.

After I had more than enough time to contemplate my future in the Army, I heard the unmistakable buzz of one of our helicopters. Making my way back to my aircraft, I awaited my fate.

Our executive officer landed his little TH-55A helicopter not far from me. He had a five-gallon can of gasoline strapped in the right seat. Exiting the aircraft, he made his way over to me carrying the can.

"You okay, Bercaw?"

"Yes, sir."

After transferring the gas to my aircraft, he started back toward his helicopter. "Just follow me."

"Yes, sir."

Looking back over his shoulder, he said, "Embarrassing, isn't it, Bercaw?"

"Yes, sir."

No one ever said another word to me about that incident.

9
Instrument Training

The great question is not whether you have failed, but whether you are content with failure.

~Chinese Proverb

May, 1967—Fort Rucker, Alabama

"John, I can't figure out what your problem is, but if you don't begin to show some improvement by tomorrow I'm going to have to recommend you for a prog ride," said my basic instrument instructor—an older civilian pilot. He never raised his voice or showed frustration, and he remained sympathetic about the whole thing. I, on the other hand, was so frustrated that it nearly brought me to tears. I wished that he would yell at me or berate me. I could handle that. His kindly tone, though, was killing me. I wanted to kick something.

I found instrument flight very difficult. I had been unable to transfer my knowledge of instrument flight to action, and panic nibbled at the back of my mind.

"John, while I'm out on the next training session use the time to think about what you're doing, and see if you can figure out what the problem is," he said.

Frank Belsky, the next student, stood beside the helicopter waiting for his turn to fly. I tried not to look too miserable as I exited the helicopter. *Now what? What the hell is my problem?* I wandered over to one of the TH-13Ts sitting on the ramp and crawled into the right seat. I was determined to sit there until I had figured out my problem, or until my instructor had returned from his training session in about one hour and forty-five minutes. The ramp's blacktop and the greenhouse-like cockpit intensified the already high temperature. I began to sweat in earnest.

Looking for a clue, I fixed my gaze on the instruments. I knew that I had a tendency to look only at the attitude indicator—a large instrument located in the middle of the instrument panel that gave the pilot a visual indication of the aircraft's attitude. It indicated whether the nose was high or low and whether the wings were level or not—all good things to know. However, the main tenet of instrument flying is that you have to verify any information that one instrument provides with the information that one or more additional instruments provide. Checking all of the instruments—a process called a crosscheck—was something that pilots did consistently throughout instrument flight, and it was exhausting work, especially for student pilots.

The Army taught new students to use a T-shaped crosscheck looking first at the instruments across the top of the panel and then looking down to see the rest of them.

It simply did not work for me.

The southern Alabama temperature and humidity continued to rise. Sweat soaked my flight suit. It was running into my eyes and making it difficult for me to see the instruments. However, I slowly worked out a new crosscheck shaped vaguely like a cloverleaf instead of a T. Starting with the attitude indicator, I made a visual sweep to the left checking the instruments in that portion of the panel. Returning to the attitude indicator, I paused and mentally analyzed all of the information that I had gained before moving visually down to the instruments in the lower portion of the panel. Once again returning to the attitude indicator, I repeated the process of analyzing the information that I had gained and integrating it with the information from the previous loop. Lastly, I made a sweep of the instruments on the right side of the panel—again repeating all the analyzing and integrating. Hopefully, at that point I would have a good idea of the flight status of the aircraft. I would need to repeat this process immediately and for the duration of each flight. Of course, I would not know if my revised crosscheck worked until I flew again the next day, but it felt a little more manageable to me, and my self-confidence received a much-needed boost.

The next day, working as hard as I had ever worked in my life, I began to gain some understanding of the process of flying an aircraft by using only the information that the instruments provided. Amazingly, I kept the aircraft under some sort of recognizable control. Upon landing the instructor looked at me curiously.

"I don't know what you're doing differently, John, but whatever it is, keep it up."

I was so relieved that I could not speak.

My skill at basic instruments continued to improve. On my check ride everything came together, and I received a very high score. I used my cloverleaf crosscheck for the remainder of my flying years.

We had all moved from Fort Wolters believing the worst was over and that Fort Rucker would be a piece of cake. It was not. The Army kept the pressure on us until we shut down the last Huey on the last day of training. Vietnam would make us appreciate this.

VIETNAM

10
Arrival Vietnam

I think that, as life is action and passion, it is required of a man that he should share the passion and action of his time at peril of being judged not to have lived.

~Justice Oliver Wendell Holmes Jr.

September, 1967—90th Replacement Depot, Long Binh (*long bin*), South Vietnam

"What the hell are you people doing in here?" yelled a young sergeant. "Get up! Get up! Formation in fifteen minutes!"

I groaned. Everyone groaned. *Crap*. Looking at my watch, I realized that I had been in bed for about an hour. I did not want to take part in any kind of formation.

"Hey, sarge, this is the officers' barracks," someone yelled.

Just out of Army helicopter flight training, I had forgotten that I was a brand new warrant officer.

"Sorry, sirs," the sergeant said. "I'm new here."

Thus began my sleep-deprived year in Vietnam.

It already seemed like a long time ago that the DC-8 carrying my fellow passengers and me had crossed over the coast of South Vietnam. We all had our faces pressed to the windows. We were anxious for a first glimpse of the land that we would call home for the next year—if we were lucky. Scattered pools of mandarin-orange light dotted the otherwise total blackness of the South Vietnam night. Someone commented that the lights came from parachute flares that the artillery had fired. I visualized a small band of brave American soldiers withstanding a horde of enemy soldiers like the British soldiers at Rorke's Drift in 1879.[3] Eventually, the lights of a city that we all assumed to be Saigon illuminated the distant horizon.

With the engines roaring and the aircraft shuddering, the pilots executed a steep and rapid approach to the runway. Peering out of the window I could see military aircraft of every type landing, departing, and taxiing. After twenty-two hours in the airplane, I wanted out. However, I had no idea what to expect. Gathering my gear and crowding into the aisle, I pushed forward toward the exit. Did combat wait just outside the plane? Who knew? As I stepped out of the door of the air-conditioned plane, hot, humid air, laced with the scents of jet exhaust and rotting vegetation welcomed me to Vietnam.

More reality came quickly. We were loaded onto military buses with chicken wire covering the windows. "What's with the wire windows?" I asked anyone.

"It's to prevent grenades from being tossed inside," responded a staff sergeant.

---

3 Depicted in the 1964 film "Zulu."

A corporal followed us onboard, and as we scrambled for seats, he briefed us about the trip to the 90th Replacement Depot at Long Binh, which was adjacent to Bien Hoa (*ben wah*).

"There will be no smoking until you reach Bien Hoa. In the event of a ground attack, which is unlikely, or a sniper attack, which is a bit more likely, stay low and the driver will drive like hell to escape."

Upon reaching our destination, soldiers herded us into a metal hut that was illuminated by rows of garish neon lights. Stand-up tables and wood planks mounted along the walls served as writing surfaces where we stood and filled out several forms between sporadic generator failures. By the time I crawled into my bunk I could no longer remember the contents of the papers I had just signed.

The new sergeant had managed to get everyone up—officers or not. The early morning light revealed depressing surroundings. Military bunk beds crowded as close as possible insured maximum occupancy of the room. An outdoor wooden toilet, still smelling of new wood, boasted four holes so there would be no waiting before you shared this intimate experience with total strangers. Designed for giants, the holes, cut so far back from the front edge of the seat that I could not bend my knees while sitting on it, made me feel like a child undergoing potty training. Fifty-five-gallon drums cut in half and partially filled with gasoline served as receptacles. This minimized smoking while using the latrine. Every morning, Vietnamese workers pulled the barrels out and set them on fire. The odor of burning feces greeted us each day. It would prove to be one of the least offensive odors I would encounter while in Vietnam. While taking a shower I realized that I had a friend. A small frog hopped around the perimeter of the dismal enclosure.

Frank Belsky and I dressed and walked outside to look for the mess hall. My new jungle fatigues served only to draw attention to the heat and humidity of the early Vietnamese morning.

Finding the mess hall, Frank and I got in line. Very quickly, a sergeant came and, despite our protestations, took us inside. Having spent five years as an enlisted man I was uncomfortable going to the head of the line. To bring the level of heat and discomfort up a notch or two we had a meal of coffee, eggs, bacon, and fried potatoes. After breakfast we wandered around the conventional military complex until we found the PX where I bought a few items: cigarettes, a small mirror, razor blades, and shaving cream. I began to relax a bit as the place seemed fairly civilized—except for the nearly constant croupy cough of artillery firing mingled with the *whomp, whomp, whomp* of helicopter rotor blades beating the air. Day and night, we heard these sounds until they became a comforting background noise, and I grew nervous when they were absent.

Numerous delicate dark-haired, dark-eyed Vietnamese women glided along the streets near the PX. They were wearing loose-fitting white pants covered by high-necked, long-sleeved, and fitted white tunics with slits along each side that extended from just above the waist. Overall, they looked elegant, demure, and very feminine. They topped off their ensembles with conical hats made of palm leaves. All of them wore some sort of open sandals ranging from flip-flops to the more typical ornate sandals. Their presence made the place seem less threatening. Vietnamese males were conspicuous by their absence.

The paper-pushers demanded a bit of our time before we could move on. Should we be wounded or killed they needed to know how we wanted our pay distributed, the names of our hometown newspapers, and how the Army should handle our affairs.

Looking around, I noticed a young warrant officer working incongruously among the other clerks.

"Who is that?" I asked, pointing at the warrant officer.

"Him? Oh, he was a pilot, but he refused to fly when he got here, and the Army assigned him to personnel duties."

"You're kidding?"

"Nope," he said, and then quickly added, "Sir."

Watching the warrant officer working with the enlisted clerks, I failed to understand how he could have gotten all the way through flight school and then refused to fly. Being a pilot is voluntary. Had he not understood the Army's plan for him? Had he no self-respect? He never looked in my direction, and I suspected that he had already weathered the contempt of many pilots who had passed through on their way to their assigned aviation duties in South Vietnam.

En route to our assignments with the 1st Infantry Division at Phu Loi (*foo loy*) Frank and I first made a stop at the 1st Division headquarters at Di An (*zee ahn*). Walking to our billets, we saw groups of soldiers marching around a large, barren open area, raising clouds of dust that blew over us.

"What are they doing?" I asked another man who was walking with us.

"Them? Oh, they spend two weeks marching, exercising, working with their weapons, and so on, so that they will become fully acclimated before being shipped out to their assigned units."

"Doesn't look like fun," I said. "I'm glad I'm not in that position."

"You guys are pilots; you won't have to do any of that."

"I hope not. I'm pretty sure we're supposed to fly around all day and spend our evenings in the bar—a bar filled with horny women. At least that is how it was explained to us when we signed up." Everyone chuckled.

Frank and I and several other soldiers were each issued an M-14 rifle when we finally departed Di An in the back of an open deuce-and-a-half. As we bounced along the dirt road feeling rather vulnerable, I asked Frank, "Did you notice that we are the ranking people here?"

He nodded.

"What are we going to do if we come under attack?" Never having been in the infantry I knew less than squat about ground fighting.

"You see that old sergeant?" Frank nodded toward a staff sergeant who was sitting on the opposite side of the truck.

I looked. He *was* old—at least thirty.

"Yes."

"I'm going to say, 'Sarge, you've got it.'"

"Good plan."

The truck driver dropped Frank off at the 1st Aviation Battalion before taking me across the runway at Phu Loi to D Troop (Air), 1st Squadron, 4th Cavalry, which was abbreviated 1/4 Cav and called the Quarter Cav. The living conditions of my new home were surprisingly nice. My assigned hootch was spacious. It had a cement floor and contained standard-issue Army beds and lockers. Screened with louvered wood strips, the walls allowed light and air in, while keeping rain and insects out. Screen doors and storm doors at each end provided additional protection from the elements. A bunker that was large enough to hold the occupants stood just outside the door. In addition, each hootch was assigned a Vietnamese woman, called a hootch maid, to clean, shine boots, and take care of laundry.

A nice mess hall and an officers' club, which the pilots and crewmembers had built, would be the scene of a mini-rebellion before long. The showers were in a separate building with a cement floor. A large barrel, cradled in stout wooden supports and painted black to help the sun warm the water, topped the building. Overall, the surroundings were rather reassuring, which was not what I had anticipated.

I expected to come to Vietnam and fly Hueys. However, I was not overly interested in killing people, and I had never made a formal request to fly gunships. As a result, I never received the gunship training in flight school.[4] I considered myself a slick[5] pilot who flew combat assaults, medevac, resupply, and rescue missions. The Quarter Cav rated a gunship platoon (call sign: Mustang), a slick platoon (call sign: Clown) and an aeroscout platoon (call sign: Outcast). Much to my surprise, each platoon desperately needed pilots and all three platoon leaders came calling wishing to recruit me.

I still did not want to fly guns, but I did consider it. The slick pilots impressed me with their skills at the controls of the old B-model Hueys. However, the aeroscout pilots got my full attention. Even cockier than the usual military pilot, most aeroscouts carried a CAR-15—a shortened version of the M-16, and I thought that they were rather cool-looking dudes. Lieutenant Dobson, the Outcast platoon leader, briefed me on the aeroscout missions. Basically, they entailed flying low and slow over the jungle while looking for the bad guys. It sounded very exciting.

---

4 My flight school class (#67-13) was the first that divided the Huey instruction into two sections, training some students as gunship pilots and the rest as slick pilots. Prior to that, all students received both types of training.

5 A slick was a Huey not rigged as a gunship and, therefore, it did not have guns and rockets hanging off the sides.

In addition, they flew OH-13S helicopters—a Korean War-era aircraft. Remembering the model that I had built at the age of seven, I made my decision. I would be an aeroscout pilot, and my call sign would be Outcast 3. However, before I began flying with the aeroscouts, I flew a mission with the Clowns.

11
Friendly Fire

The only thing more accurate than incoming enemy fire is incoming friendly fire.

~One of Murphy's Military Laws

September, 1967—First night, Phu Loi, South Vietnam

The night sky moaned as something very large raced through the heavens. Everyone was running, and I decided that I should do the same. As the last one into the bunker, I crashed into the jumble of bodies that were already crammed inside.

"Who the fuck is that?" someone said.

"It's the fucking new guy," someone else responded.

"Hey, fucking new guy, either be the first one in the bunker or take some care when entering," the first voice said.

"Sorry," I said.

Unintentionally ignoring them, I really wanted to know the source of the sound outside. It turned out to be my first encounter with incoming artillery. Unfortunately, it also turned out to be my first encounter with misdirected U.S. Army artillery, or friendly fire. Fortunately, it landed on the runway instead of on me.

And then came the explosion: *Whump.* The explosion of a large bomb consists of two parts—three, actually, as it is felt as much as heard. *Wh-ump.* The first part is an ephemeral sound, like a quick exhalation of air. This sound rolls seamlessly into the second part—a deep ground-shaking sound as the explosion smacks the earth. It is gut-shaking if you are close enough. *Whump.* This unfathomable power awakened primeval fears. *Whump.* However, the sound was mesmerizing, and the fear that it elicited became rather intoxicating. I still hear it today.

Whump.

12
FNG

You cannot create experience. You must undergo it.

~Albert Camus

September, 1967—First mission with the Clowns, Phu Loi, South Vietnam

Smoking a cigarette while leaning against the corner of my hootch, I could feel my stomach threatening to rid itself of my just-consumed breakfast of bacon, eggs, toast, and coffee. All sorts of thoughts tumbled around in my head: information I had learned in flight school that I had now seemingly forgotten; fear of the unknown; and the desire not to look completely incompetent. What did I need to know and do to make it through this day? Unfortunately, I could think of little, except for how unprepared I felt. I decided that my best course was immediate action. Tossing the cigarette, I gathered my gear and headed for my assigned UH-1B Huey helicopter. I made it to the aircraft in time to conduct the preflight inspection in the predawn light, and I had it ready for departure by the time that Captain Hudson, the platoon commander, arrived.

Initially overwhelmed by the amount of gear that the combat helicopter pilots carried, I struggled with the bulk and heat discomfort it created. We wore hot jungle fatigues that the Vietnamese laundry insisted on starching, making them even hotter and more inclined to burn if introduced to a flame—a serious consideration in a hostile environment. The inventory included jungle boots, long leather gloves, and a fitted cloth bag containing our flight helmet and other items, such as sunglasses, cigarettes, photos, and anything else deemed essential to our wellbeing. Each pilot wore a vest containing a curved ceramic plate—universally called a chicken plate—that was capable of stopping .30-caliber armor-piercing ammunition.

Pilots used the same topographical maps as the infantry, but since we covered considerably more territory, we had to assemble several maps that covered our area of operations. I had spent the previous evening taping all of my issued maps together, marking all current military positions and the locations of any wires or other obstacles that helicopters do not like. When finished I had a rather cumbersome map of approximately eight feet by ten feet. I folded it in half creating an eight-foot by five-foot map that I enclosed in a clear plastic map case. A clerk had issued me a grease pencil, along with the maps, with which to write temporary information on the plastic case. The grease, I would learn, had an unfortunate tendency to melt in the heat of Vietnam.

A small clipboard held a pad of paper, pencils, a light, and a compartment for carrying small objects. I strapped it to my left leg so that I could write instructions from air traffic control, artillery, etc.

Most pilots in the 1st Division carried a .45 caliber pistol and an M-16 rifle. All I had that morning was my .45. I noted that some pilots hung their pistols over the side of their armored seatback; I did the same.

Just aft of each pilot's door there was a small slot on the outside for placing a metal plate inscribed with the rank of the highest-ranking person onboard—seldom used, unless a general or a colonel was onboard. I found a plate on my side of the aircraft with the letters *FNG* painted on it.

"What does that mean?" I asked the crew chief.

After both he and the gunner laughed, he said, "It means Fucking New Guy."

Once everyone had arrived and we were all strapped in with the troops onboard, Captain Hudson told me to start the aircraft. In flight school we were required to memorize the checklist in the first three days after we started flying the Hueys. Therefore, I had not seen a checklist in over three months. I had not flown in about a month, and I was not certain that I could even remember how to get the thing running.

The crew chief walked around the front of the helicopter and unlatched the fire extinguisher, which was located next to my seat. That was good because I had forgotten to post a fireguard. I checked to see that the rotor blades were turned ninety degrees to the aircraft and then I focused my attention inside. Checking the flight controls for freedom of movement, I used the time to think through the startup procedure. I verified all of the circuit breakers and switches on the panel above my head and then turned the anti-collision light switch, the battery switch, the main fuel switch, and the start fuel switch to the ON positions. Then I set the altimeter.

"What's the field elevation here?"

"About ninety-five feet," someone responded.

No one said anything else to me, so I decided that everything was okay thus far. After setting the throttle, I pressed the start switch. Reassured by the turbine whine and the familiar clicking of the igniters, I relaxed a bit. The run-up was a bit tricky, as the old engine kept trying to overheat.

Captain Hudson pulled the knob that caged (stabilized) the copilot's attitude indicator, reminding me that I needed to turn the inverter switch on. After getting the engine up and running at 6,600 RPM, Hudson told me to go ahead and make the departure. I was very nervous—I had reason to be.

I pulled up on the collective lever increasing power and changing the pitch of the rotor system expecting to come to a hover. Instead, we just sat there and the old Huey began to wallow like a hog getting comfortable, throwing up a huge cloud of dust. The rotor RPM bled off to the point that the low-RPM audio came on, sending an adrenalin-producing *woo-OOP, woo-OOP, woo-OOP* into my earphones. It sounded much like the battle-station klaxons that ships use in the old WWII movies. I failed to get the helicopter off the ground, providing a great show for all of the folks in the aircraft behind me. For the next couple of days I had to endure comments about the world-class cloud of dust that I had produced. My fellow pilots would sarcastically ask me to reveal the secret for converting several gallons of jet fuel into noise, smoke, and dust.

"Let me show you how we do it here," Hudson said.

With that, he took the controls and pulled in enough power to hover under normal conditions. This made us light enough that the aircraft could slide along the ground on the skids. As we slid down the runway, I looked over my shoulder to see the rest of the formation sliding along behind us.

Once we reached translational lift—the extra lift generated by a forward airspeed of around eighteen knots—the Huey staggered into the air with its nose low. Captain Hudson held the cyclic control all the way to the rear so that it hit my belly. I scooted back in the seat to avoid it.

"We'll burn off enough fuel by the time we get to our destination that we'll have enough aft cyclic to land," Hudson said.

Landing sooner would have been very exciting. It was certainly different from the heavy-load training that I had received in flight school.

Upon reaching an altitude of 1,500 feet, Captain Hudson said, "I'm going to call artillery. Write down what they tell us."

He called for information on any artillery activity that might pose a problem for our flight. The soldier on the other end of the radio began rattling off a bunch of information that was just so much gobbledygook to me.

When finished, Hudson asked me, "What did you get?"

I showed him my blank paper. I had been twice humiliated in the space of a few minutes. Unfortunately, the day was not over.

"Take the controls and I'll get the artillery."

"I have the controls."

"You have the controls," he said, removing his hands.

We immediately fell out of the formation. The helicopter was so heavy that it required the most delicate control touch to keep it in the air. My control touch—if you could call it that—was the result of nine months of flight school in aircraft that were never anywhere near their load limits—certainly never exceeded them. I quickly learned that the phrases "weight and balance" and "maximum gross weight" were just words in a book that had very little to do with what we were doing in Vietnam. Wanting nothing more than to crawl into a hole and wait for my year to be over, I struggled to keep my control movements to an absolute minimum.

Captain Hudson was cool. He instructed one of the other aircraft to take over the lead, and we fell back so that I could practice my piloting skills. As we approached our first destination, he told me, "Take it all the way to the ground; do *not* try to bring it to a hover."

That was not going to be a problem. Our Huey was not going to hover under any circumstances. My job was to get it on the ground without bending anything. Every situation presented an opportunity to learn, and I learned then a maneuver that would serve me well in Vietnam. Setting up something that vaguely resembled a normal approach, I waited until absolute panic set in. Then I pulled in all remaining power. We touched down just as sweetly as possible.

"Not bad."

"Thank you, sir."

After much practice, I got to the point that I could make it look like I knew what I was doing.

After hot refueling, which entails keeping the engines running while refueling, we departed on our mission. We were going to conduct something called a village seal. We accomplished this by orbiting our helicopters, each one loaded with troops, around the village. Additional troops, deployed into the village just before we had arrived, looked for Viet Cong, weapons, or anything else that they could find.

In our target village, approximately thirty homes and many trees lined curving streets. Puffy clouds drifted overhead, casting the homes alternately in shade and sunlight, resulting in a pleasant movie-perfect appearance. As soon as we commenced the operation, Captain Hudson pointed to some men who were hurrying away from the village through chest-high vegetation. He took the controls and swooped down, landing less than ten feet from them. They seemed to be looking directly at me, and I realized that my pistol hung just out of reach on my seatback. This would be the last time that I ever left my pistol anywhere except on my person. As soon as we landed, the troops on our aircraft jumped out and took the men into custody.

We spent the rest of the day refueling and doing more of the same at the village. I practiced my control touch. Heading back to base at the end of the day, I spotted something familiar on the ground. Looking out of my side window, I said, "There's something down there, a shadow that looks exactly like a Huey."

"It was a Huey. It burned up," Hudson said.

"Burned up? I didn't know they burned completely," I said. "I thought a burned-out hulk would remain."

Looking a bit more carefully as we flew by, I noticed that the tips of the rotor blades that had extended out past the fire had dropped to the ground so that they lined up perfectly with the ashes. The transition from solid rotor blade to ashes was unnerving. Despite the heat, I felt a chill as these ashes disappeared behind us.

Continuing toward Phu Loi, I began to notice a putrid smell. I scrunched up my face and looked questioningly at Captain Hudson. He pointed to our right front.

I looked and saw a large elephant lying on its right side. Its skin was a leathery dark brown—almost the color of the surrounding earth. Its large white tusks gleamed in the setting sun.

"What happened to it?"

"We think the VC killed it. We all want to get the tusks, but we're afraid it's been booby trapped."

As we flew on, we passed a tree that towered above its neighbors, casting a long melancholic shadow over the surrounding jungle. Hundreds of large white birds converged on it from every direction until it looked like a large pear tree blooming white in the spring.

To this day, I cannot tell you where I was on that long mission other than somewhere in South Vietnam. I never saw the birds, the tree, the elephant, or the burned Huey again.

Humbled and more than a bit overwhelmed, I did not feel that I was a pilot; I was just some kid who had tricked the Army into letting him graduate from flight school. Now, they actually expected me to fly a helicopter in combat. In awe of the other pilots, whose skills far exceeded anything I had yet experienced in my short career as an Army Aviator, I realized that I had a lot to learn.

13
War, Adventure, and Death

Without the possibility of death, adventure is not possible.

~REINHOLD MESSNER

September, 1967—D Troop (Air), 1st Squadron, 4th Cavalry, Phu Loi, South Vietnam

It seemed like a month since I had stood and watched the pilots entering the operations building at the end of their missions, wondering what they had encountered during the day. They had been dirty, hot, and tired, but each one of them had smiled and laughed as they talked. No one appeared depressed, frightened, pissed off, or any of the attitudes that I would have expected based on all of the movies that I had seen and the books that I had read.

One of the aeroscout pilots—I could tell he was a scout pilot by the weapon he carried—had walked through the door. He was bigger and heavier than the average military pilot, who tends to be smaller in stature.

"Pete, how'd it go today?" someone yelled at him.

"Nothing. Not a damn thing. It was boring as hell," he said.

I had yet to fly a mission, and I was a bit apprehensive about what fate had in store for me. "I thought that would be a good thing," I said to the pilot who was giving me a tour of the company area.

"After a week or two here, you develop a different mind-set, and you start craving the action. It's addictive. You actually go lookin' for shit. Then just before you go home you start getting back into a stateside frame of mind, and you get all nervous again—or so I'm told."

That information was surprising. I had reentered the military partly out of a need to know how I would function in a war. However, the fact that I might actually seek out and relish combat was a novel concept.

Just a few days later and only my twelfth day in country, I found myself watching as the company commander stepped out of a truck and began walking toward me. I was wondering how much trouble was coming my way.

Two hours earlier, I had told the crew chief, who acted as the gunner in flight, that he did not need to go with me, as I intended to stay between Phu Loi and Di An. The military had flattened and destroyed every bit of vegetation between the two bases to deny the enemy hiding places. Everyone had told me that the area was secure. In reality, I had not wanted anyone around as a witness while I practiced.

During the next two hours, I practiced approaches to a farmer's field. I also practiced pedal turns and high-overhead approaches—maneuvers that I would need to be proficient with when I ventured out on my own. At one point,

I landed in the farmer's field, took a break, and smoked a cigarette.

Later, to kill time and do something different, I decided to go to Di An and shoot a low approach so that I could practice flying into another airfield and deal with an unknown tower and traffic pattern. After that, I headed back to Phu Loi to call it a day. Having ventured forth alone from my base, albeit not very far, I was feeling more confident in my abilities. Approaching the farmer's field approximately five miles south of the runway at Phu Loi, where I had earlier smoked a cigarette, I decided to execute one last landing. Setting up a nice textbook approach, I was about three feet above the ground when—*wham*—the engine backfired.

Shit. My mind raced through my training on forced landings. Realizing that I still had power, I decided to try to gain some altitude so that I would have more options if the engine decided to quit.

Wham! The ceramic plate behind my back smacked me.

Snap! Something zipped past my left ear.

Wham! Shattered Plexiglas came back and hit me in the face. *Oh, Jesus Christ, it's not the engine. Someone's shooting at me*! I ducked my head low, hoping the ceramic plate would offer protection. The plate was not big enough to shield my entire body, but it made me feel better. I could not believe it; someone was shooting at *me*. How could this be? Who was shooting? I would never know. It may have been a Viet Cong with dreams of collecting a reward for shooting down a helicopter[6] or it may have been the farmer, irritated because I kept landing in his field. Of course, it might have also been a part-time Viet Cong farmer.

---

6 We all repeated as gospel a rumor that the Viet Cong had a bounty on helicopters and helicopter pilots. However, I have never seen any documentation regarding this subject.

I pulled in all possible power and pushed the nose over to gain airspeed. The nose of the aircraft swung to the right. I pushed the left pedal to no avail; I had lost control of my tail rotor. The cyclic control began to shake. *Damn it.* I was losing my hydraulics.

"Phu Loi Tower, this is Outcast Three—an O-H-thirteen, three miles south, declaring an emergency."

"Outcast Three, this is Phu Loi. What is the nature of your emergency?"

"I was just shot up about five miles out and have lost my hydraulics and tail rotor."

"Roger, Outcast Three. You are cleared for approach. Do you require equipment to be standing by?"

"This is Outcast Three. How about if I land just to the left of the runway so that I don't tie it up? And no, I don't think I need the equipment to be standing by."

"This is Phu Loi. Roger. You are cleared as requested."

I was a bit pissed; the controller was too calm. Someone had tried to kill me, and I expected him to exhibit a bit of concern.

Everything went according to my training, except that when I touched down I completely reduced the power causing the helicopter to turn so sharply to the left that I feared it would tip over.

Had I broken any rules by flying around in that area at such a low altitude? How much trouble would I be in for having gotten the aircraft shot up? I would find out soon enough. I called our operations center.

"Darkhorse Ops, this is Outcast Three. Over."

"Darkhorse Ops, go."

"Roger. I'm sitting across the runway from you. I just got shot up and lost the tail rotor and hydraulics."

"This is Darkhorse. Roger. You okay? Over."

"I'm fine. Over."

"This is Darkhorse. Roger. Stand by. We'll send a truck."

Soon I saw a couple of trucks that were loaded with people racing across the runway to see what I had done.

Major Floyd, our commanding officer, walked over and looked around. "What altitude were you flying at, Bercaw?"

I hesitated debating what I should say.

"About five hundred feet?" he asked.

"Something like that, sir."

"Good job, Bercaw. Good job." That was my first indication that I might not be in trouble.

"Thank you, sir."

He looked the helicopter over, pausing from time to time to survey the damage.

"You had a couple rounds pass by pretty close to your head. Looks like the ceramic plate saved you," he said pointing to the plate positioned behind my back when in flight.

Later he said, "Your tail rotor control cable is severed. Looks like it happened when you had the right pedal pressed."

Finally, he said, "Here's where a round cut through the hydraulic line. Looks like a good day's work, Bercaw."

"Thank you, sir."

That afternoon, I went into the local town and got drunk. My good luck began to sink in after a couple of drinks. I was alive because the shooter had been too quick on the trigger. This would not be the only time in Vietnam that I would survive because of the enemy's impatience. Thank God for ceramics — at the very least, this kept me from being wounded. Smoking the cigarette in the farmer's field had been dangerous and stupid, as was my telling the tower that I did not need emergency equipment.

Nevertheless, with all things considered, I was rather pleased with myself. I had lost my combat virginity and I now fancied myself a combat veteran. I had entered a new phase for my year in Vietnam. I soon developed the bullet-proof mentality and the cockiness that most military pilots exhibit. I was good and my fight was righteous, and these qualities would carry me through my year—or so I thought. I began seeking action so that I could prove just how good I was. When action came and I emerged unscathed, this reinforced my opinions about my abilities. Some men died, and this added to my evolving frame of mind. I was no longer satisfied with just being good. To validate my status as a combat pilot I needed the very real possibility of death along with the opportunity to cheat it. And I have been nothing in my life if not a good combat pilot.

14
First Death

They shall grow not old, as we that are left grow old;
Age shall not weary them, nor the years condemn.
At the going down of the sun and in the morning
We will remember them.

~Laurence Robert Binyon

September, 1967—Michelin Rubber Plantation, vicinity of Lai Khe (*lie kay*), South Vietnam

His body hit the floor of the helicopter with multiple thumps as different bones and then his head struck the metal plates. It sounded like nothing more than a large bag of potatoes dropping on the floor. As the pilot commenced takeoff, I looked out my door squinting against the early morning sun. I saw the backs of the two men who had placed the dead soldier in the aircraft. They ran through the tall grass – back to relative safety far away from our large, noisy presence.

Not knowing what to expect, I forced myself to look back at the soldier's crumpled body. It looked as if someone had piled dirty laundry behind my seat. His face and hands were as dirty as his uniform. They all blended visually making it difficult to realize that this was a human body. His face seemed peaceful; his eyes were closed. Something was wrong, however. I did not see any blood or wounds.

"He was shot in the head, sir," the crew chief said.

Eventually I spotted one small wound just above his left temple. Perfectly round it looked as if it had been put there with a hole punch. There was no blood, but a small amount of white material blocked the opening.

"That's his brains." The crew chief again correctly guessed my thoughts.

"He looks so small."

"Everyone does," the pilot said. "They fall down and their uniform looks way too big. They look almost flat—like the earth has already started to reclaim them."

"He doesn't look real," I said, still transfixed by the sight of this dead soldier.

"That's one thing the movies can't do. They can't make actors look dead the way a body does when all life has gone. And people don't go through all the contortions when they get shot that the movie folks do. When you get fatally shot, you just drop. Bang. You drop. You're dead."

"How do you know this?"

"I spent about nine months over here in the infantry with the Cav. I decided that pilots had it made and applied for flight school. Took the exams right down in Saigon, went straight back to flight school, and here I am again."

"Lucky you."

"Trust me; compared to being a grunt, this ain't bad."

Taking a last look at the soldier on the floor, I decided that he would almost certainly agree with that statement.

15
BDA

Results are what you expect, and consequences are what you get.

~SCHOOLGIRL'S DEFINITION, QUOTED IN *LADIES' HOME JOURNAL* (JANUARY, 1942)

October, 1967—Somewhere over the South Vietnamese jungle

Bomb craters seemed to dot the entire South Vietnamese countryside. One country or another had been fighting in Vietnam for years – decades even – but it was hard to imagine that during those years soldiers had fought on literally every inch of terrain. The very idea was overwhelming.

The craters, created by exploding bombs or artillery shells, quickly filled with water soon richly colored by the chemicals from the explosive device. This resulted in milk-chocolate browns, hunter greens, milky whites, dull blood reds, and turquoise blues. Sometimes the holes overlapped resulting in an expanded color palette. Cradled by the emerging verdant shoots in the rice paddies, it was like looking down on opened cans of paint sitting in the grass.

Long slashes of bomb craters crisscrossed the country—the results of B-52 Arc Light strikes. Conducted night and day these attacks felt like earthquakes and sounded like thunder. Everyone who happened to view one agreed that it was an overwhelming display of man's destructive powers. The Outcast pilots sometimes flew Bomb Damage Assessment, or BDA, missions to assess the resultant damage.

Orbiting about five miles from the designated target in my OH-13, I was excited about conducting my first BDA. But when the strike came, I observed a vengeful beast of fire and oily black smoke stomping across the landscape. A white-hot flash with a rapidly expanding white shock ring marked each step like ripples on water. Feeling chilled the hairs on my arms and legs stood on end. The smoke and dust rose above our altitude of a thousand feet above the ground. The B-52s, unseen by us, continued back to their home bases far from the war.[7]

Turning toward the wall of smoke and dust that drifted slowly away to the east Lieutenant Dobson began a rapid descent toward the destroyed landscape. I followed uncertain of what to expect. However, I knew that if any soldiers had survived they would be more than a little upset.

We dropped down into a large open area until we were below the tops of the trees and could look back into the jungle for a short distance. First, the sight of footprints in

7 For the B-52 flight crews, the war must have been a very boring experience. However, they would be back to their base in the Philippines or Thailand in time for happy hour, and since they had actually spent a few minutes over South Vietnam they were able to draw their combat pay for the month—but I digress.

the fresh bomb craters astonished me. People had survived. Second, I took one breath and gagged. Unable to breathe, I felt a moment of panic.

"Outcast Three, this is Outcast Six. Breathe through your mouth," Dobson informed me.

The ferocity of the bomb blasts had shredded the jungle foliage into fine pieces—almost a mist—resulting in a chlorophyll stench that now assaulted my respiratory system. I had difficulty breathing during the entire time I was in that area.

Third, as I dropped down below the surrounding trees into one of the bomb craters, I belatedly realized that my aging helicopter did not have enough power to maintain a high hover in Vietnam's heat and humidity. I found myself slowly settling down into a hole created by one of the bomb blasts. The eighty-foot trees presented a very formidable barrier. With the crew chief guiding me I backed up as far as possible to provide a takeoff run long enough to accelerate through translational lift. Then using every ounce of power I could coax out of the engine—and a control touch that was considerably more delicate than I had exhibited on my first mission—we slowly climbed out of an embarrassing and dangerous situation.

Numerous square holes that were now exposed might have been fighting positions or perhaps storage containers. The occasional remains of a building were visible on the periphery of the blast areas—and so were those damned footprints. The intelligence that had directed the air strike had apparently been correct. We failed to locate the individuals who had made the footprints, and a part of me rejoiced that anyone could survive such destruction. Whoever they were, as far as I was concerned, they had earned the right to live another day.

16
The Kill

There's a destructive urge in people, the urge to rage, murder, and kill.

~ANNE FRANK

Late 1967—Vicinity of Phu Loi, South Vietnam

We attacked at dawn one fine day in late 1967—before any people would be present. As I flew toward one of the animals, the gunner leaned out of the door and opened fire on full automatic. Some animals dropped, but most ran away their bodies riddled with bullets. It turned out that water buffalo were very difficult to kill.

Our mission, a shit mission most likely dreamed up by some rear echelon bureaucrat who was trying to justify his existence and his safe job, involved killing those buffalo belonging to suspected Viet Cong sympathizers.

A small herd of the creatures inhabited a large rice paddy. They proved to be too much for us, so we called in the gunships. They rolled in and unleashed a hellish mixture of mini-gun fire, rockets, and grenades, causing the rice paddy to erupt in a fountain of fire, smoke, mud, water, and blood. The buffaloes, eyes white with fear, closed into a tight defensive huddle and as a unit made a slow counter-clockwise turn in a futile attempt to avoid the hell men directed toward them. At the completion of the gun run, those water buffalo that were still standing all ran away.

Eventually, after repeated gun runs—long after all chatter had ceased on the radios and there was enough butchery to sate even the most bloodthirsty—all of the buffalo lay dead or dying, except for one lone creature that was standing in the middle of a small rice paddy. At the east end stood a small grove of tall trees that were casting long shadows and providing shade from the early morning sun. The buffalo, unfazed by the carnage that had been going on around it, ate contently. Placing its muzzle into the water, it pulled up a mouthful of grass, ate, took a step or two, and ate some more.

My wingman made a run to kill it. His gunner leaned out and commenced firing straight down into the rice paddy. A deadly trail of closely spaced water splashes—marking the impacts made by the bullets—moved closer to the ill-fated animal, and then walked over its hindquarters severing the spine. Its back legs collapsed. The water buffalo, bawling so loudly that I could hear it over the roar of the engine, dragged itself through the rice paddy using its front legs and watched me as I flew low overhead. Unfortunately, a lack of ammunition prevented us from completing the kill.

Sometimes, when the night is darkest, I can hear the cries of fear and pain echoing down through the decades as that ghostly beast drags itself through the water and the mud, its hind legs trailing uselessly behind—and those eyes watch me.

17
Mountain Woman

Beauty is everywhere a welcome guest.

~JOHANN VON GOETHE

Late 1967—Somewhere in the mountains northeast of Song Be (*song bay*), South Vietnam

"What the hell are they looking at?" my door gunner asked.

"I dunno."

Lieutenant Dobson's OH-13 had been orbiting the same spot for a long time. It was too far away for me to see what he was looking at, but I could see some Montagnard[8] buildings a short distance up the mountain from where his aircraft circled.

8 French for "mountain dweller" and pronounced *mon-tuhn-yahrd*. They are indigenous people inhabiting the mountains and highlands of southern Vietnam. Regarded as savages and hated by the Vietnamese, they were extremely loyal to U.S. forces. At the end of the war, the United States abandoned them. The Vietnamese still persecute them today.

"Outcast Six, what have you got?" I called on the radio.

"This is Six. Stand by."

"Whatever it is, it must be interesting," said the gunner.

"I'm assuming it's not people, or he wouldn't expose himself like that. It's probably some bunkers or something like that," I said.

"Okay, we're done here," Dobson finally called as he made a turn to the north and away from the area.

I should have followed him, but my curiosity got the best of me, and I diverted over to the spot that he had been circling.

Walking with a precision that looked almost military, a young Montagnard woman proceeded up a well-worn trail that led from the jungle to a small village situated on top of the mountain.

She kept a constant eye on us as we flew around her. Her clothing consisted of nothing except for a kind of loincloth wrapped around her waist and between her legs. Her long, thick hair, held back from her face in a full ponytail, descended to her waist. She was all roundness and curves with dark dusty skin. Her breasts were high and firm. Her hips were pleasantly full. Seemingly unafraid—even arrogant—she watched us with her head held back and her chin jutted out.

"I'm betting she's the daughter of the chief," I said.

"Jesus, she's beautiful. She could be in Playboy," said the gunner.

And she was beautiful—stunningly so. I wanted to take the same amount of time Dobson had and watch her walk, but his aircraft was disappearing to the north, and I needed to catch up. Reluctantly I broke off and sped after him. I saw her for no more than a minute or two, but her image—one of the more pleasant images I had in Vietnam—lingers still.

18
Fish Hook

Let me assert my firm belief that the only thing we have to fear is fear itself.

~Franklin D. Roosevelt

October, 1967—Along the Cambodian border slightly southwest of Loc Ninh (lock nin), South Vietnam

"Gooooooood morning, Vietnam!" The disc jockey in Saigon greeted the sun as it peeked over the horizon.

Somewhere in the air over South Vietnam an anonymous, disgruntled pilot tuned to the emergency frequency and broadcast, "Fuck Vietnam."

It was the same every morning.

Only this morning was not the same. My breakfast, a churning lump in my stomach, made me regret that I had tried to eat at all. The coffee had been bitter and the cigarettes tasted like shit. The briefing the previous evening had emphasized that our mission would be in an area with a triple-canopy jungle and a high concentration of bad guys. We were going to reconnoiter around an area called the Fish Hook—a name given to the outline on our maps where the Cambodian border extended about five kilometers into South Vietnam. This gave the enemy a staging area that was well inside our territory. From there they could launch attacks. I thought it looked more like the outline of Florida.

Everyone was on edge.

I wondered what being shot would feel like. Would it be a burning sensation or would it be like something heavy striking my body—or both? Regardless of the risk I was determined to do my job and not let the unit down. I also did not want to appear to be afraid. Only half-joking military pilots said that it was better to die than to sound bad on the radio. Over drinks in the evening we joked about anyone who had let his voice travel up a few octaves during a tense situation. I did not intend to fall into that category.

After a quick refueling stop at Loc Ninh, we headed west to the border. Upon reaching our designated area I followed the lead OH-13 as we made a rapid descent to an altitude of about ten feet above the dense jungle. Any problem in this area that required an immediate landing—an engine failure, for example—would most likely result in the destruction of the aircraft and the deaths of the crewmembers. Even if they survived, a rescue mission would be a major undertaking.

We swept back and forth across our assigned territory. To provide proper coverage for the lead aircraft I had to fly across the border into Cambodia from time to time. Less than one hundred yards inside Cambodia, I looked down through the jungle and nearly had a coronary. I saw what appeared to be an entire town hidden beneath the jungle roof—complete with streets.

"This is Outcast Three. I've got buildings all over the place down here. Jesus Christ. Some of them are two stories."

"Outcast Three, you are on the wrong side of the red line."

What? I did not understand what the caller—I think it was our commanding officer—meant.

"This is Outcast Three," I said. "Say again."

"Look at your map. You're on the wrong side of the border."

I knew that.

"I know that. Can't we call in an air strike? Jesus Christ. This is a bonanza."

"Negative on that, and try to stay on this side of the red line."

"Roger that."

Now I was pissed. My gunner was pissed, and everyone in the flight was probably pissed. What bullshit. The enemy had built their town just a few yards across the border in Cambodia allowing them to come and go at will, and we just let them.

"Fucking politicians. Fucking candy-ass, chicken-shit, no-balls sons of bitches," I said.

"What do they care? They're not here," the crew chief replied.

We kept up the recon. As we crisscrossed the border the constant tension-relaxation cycle eventually began to wear me down. I became so exhausted that I allowed myself to become more pissed off because it was easier on my nervous system.

"I almost wish they would open fire on us," I said. "Then we could shoot the place up."

"They won't do that," the crew chief said. "They have nothing to gain and everything to lose."

We just kept flying hoping to spot something worthwhile on our side of the border, even though there was little chance of that happening. It would have made no sense for them to build on our side when safety was just steps away.

"This is Outcast Six. We're finished here."

"This is Dark Horse Six," said our commanding officer over the radio. "Roger. We're heading back." I looked up to see his Huey break off and head for home.

"Outcast Six, this is Mustang One-Niner. We're heading back also," the lead gunship pilot called as they broke off and headed back.

That was it. I cruised along the border looking at the buildings and feeling cheated.

"Sir, can I shoot them up?" my gunner asked.

"Fucking A," I said. "Open fire."

He commenced firing his M-60 machine gun into the jungle in the direction of the buildings as I flew parallel to the border. When he ran out of ammo, I made a quick exit to the east.

"Watch this." The gunner pointed to the gunships, which were high overhead.

The two helicopters above had swung back around and were heading west. Like a deadly ballet both helicopters rose gracefully into a nose-high position and fired off all of their rockets in the direction of Cambodia. It was a very satisfying sight. I tried to imagine the rockets slamming down in the midst of some surprised Viet Cong and North Vietnamese Army personnel who were certain that they were safe in their Cambodian sanctuary. All things considered, it was a good day.

19
Marvin the Arvin

When I hear somebody sigh, "Life is hard," I am always tempted to ask, "Compared to what?"

~**Sydney J. Harris**

Late 1967—ARVN compound near Saigon, South Vietnam

Ducking my head as I stepped through the open door and out of the intense midmorning sunlight, I paused until my eyes adjusted to the gloominess inside. Two small windows lit the room—one in the far wall and the other in the wall to my left. This made it even more difficult to see the interior. The windows had no glass or screens. The only other light filtering into the room came from the door, and I blocked most of that. Four wooden tables with straight-back wooden chairs occupied more than half of the small room where I was to wait while Lieutenant Dobson attended a briefing.

Three ARVN soldiers occupied the table that most benefited from the cross-ventilation of the two windows. They sat smoking and drinking soft drinks. Wooden storage cabinets stood to the right of the door and a small counter stood to the left. I scanned the selection of Vietnamese snacks behind the counter and recognized none. A cooler contained a selection of soft drinks. I ordered a bottled Coke from the old woman who was minding the store.

As my eyes adjusted to the contrasting lighting conditions, I moved toward the nearest open table. The floor changed colors as I walked. Perhaps my eyes had not fully adjusted and they were playing tricks on me. I looked down to see that the floor was literally covered in flies—big, fat flies that did not and possibly could not fly. There were so many flies that they appeared to be a black carpet—a moving black carpet. Like water, they flowed out in front of me and closed in again behind me as I walked.

Fearful that I would step on them, I paused. However, when I stopped the flies crawled closer to my boots retaking the space that they had allotted to me while I had been walking. The Vietnamese soldiers watched me, and I forced myself to move forward to the table. Flies also covered the table and chair, but they moved away to give me a large enough area to sit down. I took a drink, set the Coke bottle on the table, and removed my hand. Like some science-fiction blob set on devouring everything in its path, the flies immediately swarmed up the sides of the bottle until it was just a black object that happened to be shaped like a Coke bottle—a small black Coke bottle that constantly moved. I never touched it again. Apparently, the Board of Health had not made their annual visit that year—probably something to do with the contingencies of war and all that.

I sat looking outside trying to avoid eye contact with the soldiers and longing to lunge for the door and the freedom that it offered from this fly-infested hell. I felt certain that they were crawling over me and eating my flesh. All that the lieutenant would find when he returned would be my thoroughly cleaned skeleton and possibly my belt buckle. I probably did not have anything to worry about, as the flies obviously had plenty to eat without devouring a living creature.

Desperate to escape, I pondered how long before I could leave without offending anyone. Fortunately, the lieutenant returned earlier than expected. He motioned to me indicating that I should accompany him. I was so relieved that I could have hugged him.

Escorted further into the ARVN compound, we passed through what appeared to be the housing area for the South Vietnamese enlisted men and their families. They had used whatever available material they could find to construct the individual buildings. The rusted corrugated tin that they used for the roofs and windowless walls seemed to be in plentiful supply. Occasionally, I saw discarded wooden pieces mixed into the construction of a few buildings. Some huts stood alone, while some joined with others in a visually disturbing apartment complex based on no known architectural principles.

Not one thing grew in this area of bare, hard dirt—not even a rugged weed. Dust swirled around the people and the buildings. I assumed it also went inside the buildings. Almost everyone squatted Vietnamese style in the little shade that the tin huts provided. The interiors of the buildings must have been hellish infernos. A few children, some of them smoking cigarettes, played in the dirt. A few women listlessly tried to wash clothing in small pans of dirty water. I spotted very few soldiers. I assumed that they were out doing soldierly things. Desolation, despair, and depression had found a home.

We passed through a guarded gate in a fence constructed of multiple strands of razor-sharp concertina wire. Dobson disappeared inside a windowless building with our escort, leaving me outside with no instructions. I observed several square holes in the ground, the nearest one being about thirty feet away from me. Iron bars, like the bars on jail cells in old western movies, lay over each hole. Curious, I walked over to one and was surprised to see a man at the bottom looking up at me. The hole was just that, an eight- to ten-foot square hole that someone had dug to a depth of ten or twelve feet. It contained a lone male and nothing else. I walked over to another hole and saw that it too held a man. Both men looked to be Vietnamese. At that point, an armed Vietnamese soldier approached, motioning with his M-16 rifle that I should return to the building. I did.

Later another Vietnamese soldier came out of the building and stopped to light a cigarette. He spoke to me in halting English and asked how I was.

"I'm fine," I said. "Who are the men in the holes?"

"They Viet Cong. Sometimes American soldier bring man, put in hole." He smiled and walked away.

A bit later, the lieutenant walked from the building into the bright hot sun. "Let's go," he said.

I was only too happy to oblige.

20
Bu Dop

No gallant action was ever accomplished without danger.

~John Paul Jones

Late November, 1967—En route to Bu Dop (*boo dop*), South Vietnam

As Lieutenant Dobson and I departed Quan Loi (*kwan loy*) and headed north to Bu Dop, we observed an Air Force fast mover swooping down like a hawk on an unfortunate mouse. At about five hundred feet above the ground, the pilot released a bomb, and then pulled the aircraft's nose up, kicked in the afterburners, and zoomed back to altitude in just seconds as we chugged along at about sixty-five knots. The bomb's explosion sent a white shock wave skimming across the tops of the trees. Almost immediately, a second jet dropped down from the heavens, trailing little puffs of smoke from the cannons it fired into the pervasive jungle below. Scattered white flashes sparkled all around the target area reminding me of twinkling Christmas lights.

We had the best seats in the house for observing the show. Each pilot broke to the left at the completion of his run, climbing to altitude in a wide left turn to allow spacing between the aircraft. However, as we passed very close to the target area, one of the pilots broke to the right bringing his aircraft screaming around and heading straight for Lieutenant Dobson's helicopter. Fortunately, the Air Force pilot spotted the OH-13 and flipped his plane from a right-wing-down position to a left-wing-down position. It was now heading straight for me. Spotting my helicopter, he pushed the nose of his aircraft forward and passed between Lieutenant Dobson and myself. There was just enough room for his jet. I could clearly see the eyes of the pilot looking straight up at me through his canopy. My helicopter bounced through the turbulence the jet had created. This happened in mere seconds. I barely had time to become concerned.

Having flown ahead, our gunships waited for us at Bu Dop, a small base consisting of a short, narrow runway that was little better than dirt. The refueling points, based along the side of the runway next to the perimeter, presented lucrative targets to any enemy hiding outside. Upon landing, I spotted an unexploded mortar round sticking in the ground about fifteen feet away. I was surprised that the rotor wash from our helicopters had not set it off.

Enemy soldiers had overrun the perimeter at Bu Dop the previous evening. The artillery crews had lowered their cannons and fired straight into the enemy forces using flechette rounds—nasty antipersonnel rounds containing approximately 10,000 small-finned steel darts that spread in a very effective and extremely devastating pattern. Word of the battle had filtered down to us the previous evening and though not scheduled to fly the next day, I asked for the mission. A rumor we all wanted to believe said that the war was going to end soon, and I thought I wanted to see some real action before that happened.[9]

As we refueled, an Air Force C-130 came into view on a long final approach for the little airstrip. Somewhat surprised, I did not think the runway was large enough for an aircraft that big and heavy, I stopped working to see what it was going to do. The C-130's crew had lowered the aft loading ramp. As it approached the end of the runway, an enemy .51-caliber machine gun opened fire. The big aircraft touched down at the exact beginning of the runway, which was only as wide as the landing gear.

As soon as the wheels hit the ground, a parachute popped out of the back, pulling a large pallet of equipment out of the rear of the aircraft. The pallet hit the runway with a loud crash and a lot of dust. Another pallet immediately followed with another crash and more dust. With its engines roaring, the C-130 continued with what was essentially a touch-and-go landing, and then it departed the airfield. Another .51-caliber weapon began firing as it departed. The entire operation took twenty seconds or less. Swarms of men I had not previously noticed ran from shacks along the runway and began moving the pallets. They were not American, and I really hoped they

9 Eventually, we learned that the attack on Bu Dop was one of several preliminary battles leading up to the Tet Offensive in 1968.

were not members of the same group that had fired on the C-130.[10]

After refueling, the first task we were given was to locate the enemy .51-caliber weapons. I loved the concept of sending a small, slow Korean War vintage helicopter out looking for weapons that could easily bring down jets. Off we went with Lieutenant Dobson in the lead flying about two feet above the tops of the trees. Slowly, he pulled away from me. I increased the power and sped up until my airspeed reached the red line and then went a bit beyond, but he was still running away from me.

"Outcast Six, this is Outcast Three," I radioed to Dobson. "You need to slow down because I can't keep up with you."

"Do your best."

I understood his concern. If we spotted any large weapons, or if the enemy spotted us first, he wanted to make certain that they did not have time to target us. I agreed with this, but I could not do a good job providing immediate suppressive fire from this far back. As I made a good secondary target that the enemy could prepare for, I flew a slightly different route.

A .51-caliber weapon opened fire. We easily heard its throaty noise—*boom, boom, boom*—over the engine noise.

"Taking fire. Taking hits!" someone yelled through my earphones.

---

10 C-130s seemed to be almost as numerous as helicopters in Vietnam. They operated in many of the same areas that we did and were highly desirable targets of opportunity for the enemy. I watched them operate in areas that were essentially trails with the nearest trees removed to accommodate the wings. On departure, the pilots would run the engines up to full RPM, release the brakes, and become airborne in an astonishingly short distance. I developed an enormous respect for the brave and skillful pilots and crewmembers of these aircraft.

I glanced at the crew chief. He looked at me with wide and wild eyes, and then he turned abruptly and began firing out the door. My stomach muscles knotted so violently that for a moment I thought I might have taken a hit.

"This is Outcast Three. Taking fire!" I yelled over the radio, thinking that the crew chief had been the one to make the first transmission. The noise from the gunner's M-60 hurt my ears and probably drowned out my transmission.

"All aircraft return and land," someone called. I believe it was Major Floyd, our commanding officer. Adrenalin was the stimulant of the moment.

"What happened?" I asked the crew chief.

"Didn't you say we were taking fire?" he responded.

"No. I heard the guns and thought you made the call," I replied.

Okay, I thought. *This is going to be embarrassing.* I had radioed that we were taking fire, but apparently, we were not. Another aircraft was.

Upon landing, we discovered that one of the gunship pilots had made the call. They had taken fire and one of the rounds had come up through the floor on the pilot's side where it penetrated the fire extinguisher causing it to explode. The pilots lost all visibility in the cockpit. They fell nearly to treetop level before regaining control.

As we stood there talking, two additional gunships landed on the other side of the runway. The first pilot out, Frank Belsky, headed across the runway. Hunched over like a boxer taking short, quick strides, his piercing dark eyes were clearly visible. He seemed like a very menacing character as he advanced.

"You stupid son-of-a-bitch!" He raised his arm, pointing his index finger straight at me.

"What's wrong?" I began backing away. Although not a large man, Frank was a tough street fighter and he could be very intimidating when he was angry.

"We're in a duel with a quad 50, and you flew right through my gun line." He was in my face now. "I almost blew your ass out of the sky!"

"What? Frank. What? I'm sorry. I didn't know you were even in the area."

"I was yelling at you on the emergency frequency!"[11]

"Frank, I'm sorry. The radios were all going crazy, and we had a bit of a situation going on ourselves. I'm sorry."

"Well, pay more attention, you stupid shit. I'd hate to have to tell your wife that I'm the one who killed you."

"Okay. Okay, I will. And you take care of yourself, too."

The day had just begun.

---

11 I never heard his radio call, as the gunships used the UHF emergency frequency of 243.0. The OH-13s did not have UHF radios and used the VHF emergency frequency of 121.5.

21
New Year's Eve

I am convinced that life is 10% what happens to me and 90% how I react to it.

~CHARLES SWINDOLL

December 31, 1967—Officers Club, D Troop (Air), 1/4 Cav, Phu Loi, South Vietnam

The Quarter Cav Officers' Club would be the scene of a mini-rebellion in the dark hours of January 1, 1968. Notified earlier that we would have a stand-down New Year's Day, which meant that we would fly no missions, everyone was looking forward to relaxing and some serious partying on New Year's Eve. As missions ended that day, men cleaned up and headed to the bar. The drinking began early, and it would continue all night.

Around dusk Major Moore, our executive officer, led several non-flying officers, all majors and above who were unknown to any of the pilots, into the club, along with several young women who worked with Martha Raye in her show.

Our squadron commander, a colonel, had recently appropriated the club, which had once been the off-duty hangout for pilots. Previously, when a pilot returned to the states he hung his hat, which had his call sign embroidered on the back, on the wall opposite the door. A special section contained the hats of all the Quarter Cav pilots killed in Vietnam. The colonel had ordered these removed. In their place, he hung framed copies of the Cav song. The commandeering of our sanctuary irritated all of the pilots, especially those who had devoted many hours of sweat equity into building it.

We had seen very few women and no round-eyed women, except for the occasional Donut Dolly. To say we had some interest in our female visitors would be an understatement. Unfortunately, the women would have nothing to do with the warrant officer pilots, and one of the pilots said he heard them making disparaging remarks about us. This, of course, did not go over well. After all, we knew we were superior to desk jockeys and other REMFs. This situation added another irritation to our growing list.

Lines were drawn. The interloper officers and the women sat on one side of the room at the dining tables, while the pilots hung around the bar. Alcohol flowed, irritation increased, and an unspoken plan began to unfold. We would be especially offensive so that no one would enjoy the evening. The plan would be very successful.

We told loud, expletive-laden stories that involved all sorts of military exploits designed to shock the non-combatants. Obscene stories, the more obscene, the better, followed. Everyone on our side of the room followed each story with loud and intentionally obnoxious guffaws.

At midnight, the entire Phu Loi perimeter interrupted our activities by erupting briefly in a spontaneous celebration involving gunfire. We all ran outside of the club to witness tracers climbing high into the sky as the men who were on guard duty that night welcomed 1968 with their own fireworks.

Around two in the morning, someone decided that we should all sing the despised Cav song. Each warrant officer sang it at the top of his voice, and we ended with a hearty chorus of, "Fuck the Cav!" Each of us then hurled our glass, full or not, at the framed song. Ice, liquids, and broken glass flew in all directions, amid cheers and more obscenities. It was a wonderful end to the evening—at least for me.

Around that time, our commanding officer, Major Floyd, informed me that I had a six o'clock mission.

"Sir, I thought we had a stand down."

"We did, but I've been requested to field one ship for a reconnaissance mission."

"Sir, I'm drunk."

"So is everyone else."

After two or three hours of sleep, I crawled into my uniform, gathered my gear, and trudged off to the helicopter in the early morning light of the first day of 1968. The crew chief was already there. We both looked and felt like shit.

We were to conduct a simple road recon prior to sending a group of American vehicles down it. One of our helicopters reconnoitered that dusty road every morning. It led back to a lonely firebase, and no one but military forces used it. I maintained about fifty knots, while making S turns back and forth from one side of the road to the other looking for anything suspicious. Cleared of vegetation for about one hundred yards on each side, the road was not likely to be the scene of a traditional ambush, but mines and buried bombs were an ever-present danger. Our troops traveled it every day.

As I approached the tree line on the south side of the road and prepared to make a turn back to the north, I heard a strange wailing sound. *What the hell*? Was something weird happening to the engine? I darted back over the road so I would have a smooth hard surface on which to land should the engine quit. I glanced at the crew chief for an explanation. He hung limply out the side of the helicopter. I thought he was dead. Suddenly, his head snapped up and he lunged backward into the helicopter, sucking as much air into his lungs as he could. This caused the wailing noise. Once his lungs filled, he again hurled himself forward in a rather spectacular demonstration of dry heaves, as his body tried to rid itself of all the alcoholic poison consumed the previous evening.

I immediately slowed the aircraft and stopped all abrupt maneuvers. "Jesus. I'm sorry, chief."

He leaned back, pale, sweating, and breathing heavily. I slowly turned the aircraft around and headed back. Mission over.

When I returned to base, Major Moore called a formation for all of the warrant officers. For some reason the major felt that we had insulted him and his guests. After first challenging each of us to a fight, he likened us to children and informed us that we were not officers—just officer trainees. He further informed us of the special classes he had arranged for the warrants so we could learn how to be officers. We were to attend these classes any time we were not actually on a mission.

Fuck him. Recently notified that the Army wanted me transferred to the 101st Airborne Division, I did not give a shit about his classes or his wounded pride.[12] I was leaving, and now I felt better about that.

---

12 Major Moore makes another appearance in Hugh Mill's excellent book *Low Level Hell*, published by Presidio Press.

22
101st

We see the brightness of a new page where everything yet can happen.

~RAINER MARIA RILKE

Early January, 1968—Company A, 101st Aviation Battalion, 101st Airborne Division, Bien Hoa, South Vietnam

Already unhappy about my assignment to a new and untested unit, I arrived at the 101st area in Bien Hoa one cool, overcast morning to find all the A Company warrant officer pilots segregated into a single open-bay building of rough unpainted wood. Filled with footlockers and army cots with two or three feet of space between them, it reminded me of the Quonset hut I had lived in while I was still a low-ranking enlisted Marine on Okinawa. Awnings over small windows kept out both the worst of the weather and any natural light. A few bare light bulbs hanging down from the peaked ceiling struggled to hold the intrinsic gloom at bay. Having all the charm of a coal shed, the building did nothing to improve my sour mood. Before my year was over, I would find myself living in a tent, in a tarpaulin-covered hole in the ground, and frequently, my helicopter provided my accommodations for the night. I found all of this to be preferable to that wretched building at Bien Hoa.

Worse, the feeling of brotherhood that the warrant officers and officers in my old unit shared, with the exception of the XO, was not evident in the 101st. Warrant officers clearly were considered a nuisance necessitated by the exigencies of the war. Worse still, the warrant officers were a rather sullen bunch, seemingly having accepted the rather plebeian opinion that the rest of the company had of them. In the Quarter Cav, officers, with few exceptions, flew regular missions alongside the warrants. This included the commanding officer and the executive officer. This would not be the case in the 101st.

New names had to be associated with new faces: Morgan, Overstreet, Fritz, Narburgh, Smith, Mays, Neal, Hagan, Wold, and a host of others whose names I have forgotten. After having flown the OH-13S almost exclusively for the previous three months, I now had to make the transition to the UH-1H Huey and a different type of mission. None of this thrilled me.

One of the first pilots with whom I became acquainted was Jim Morgan. Most of us considered Jim a bit of an eccentric. Jim had scrounged some plywood that he nailed to the support posts, creating a small room that was larger than the space allocated to each pilot. His young wife Joan sent him tapes of various rock-and-roll songs, and he played these while he continued the construction of his semi-private abode. Between songs, Joan talked, often saying things that newlyweds say to each other. We were all amused when Jim rushed to the tape recorder at the end of each song to try to turn the volume down before she started talking. Sometimes, he would not make it—much to our delight.

I ended up flying more hours with Jim while in Vietnam than with any other pilot, and having shared the experiences that only combat can provide, we became life-long friends.

Thankfully, my time at Bien Hoa was short-lived. I moved north soon after the beginning of Tet, and I never returned until I began my trip back home. I never missed it.

23
Shall I Shoot Him, Sir?

Trust not too much to appearances.

~Virgil

January, 1968—Song Be, South Vietnam

Prior to Tet '68, our platoon kept an aircraft based at Song Be most of the time. The hours were long. The work was dirty. Sleeping arrangements were in the red dirt or in the aircraft. Bathing was non-existent, and food consisted of C-Rations. We were on-call twenty-four hours a day. However, some of the pilots and many of the enlisted men preferred it this way as they were on their own and did not have to put up with the bullshit associated with the rear areas.

During one of my stays late in January, enemy activity had picked up, and we were busier than usual. On about our third day, we began flying at dawn, and we flew all of that day. Then we flew missions off and on throughout most of the night only to find ourselves back in the air early the next morning. I did not shut the aircraft down until late afternoon. At that time, my crew and I opened some C-Rations for a quick meal before we were called on to fly some more. We were all exhausted, dirty, and unshaven. I was so hungry I was shaking. The ubiquitous red laterite, crushed into a powder so fine that it flowed like water away from our feet when we walked, coated all of us from head to foot. Even the helicopter's olive-drab paint now had a reddish hue.

As we ate, I noticed a major standing about fifty yards away watching us. He was wearing pressed jungle fatigues—*pressed* jungle fatigues—and his boots, although dusty, were polished. Wonderful. A REMF major was at one of our forward bases with nothing more to do than watch us eat.

Before long, he walked smartly over to our location.

"Who is in command here?"

"I am, major," I said.

"What are you doing?"

I thought that was rather obvious, but I said, "We're eating, major." I refused to call him "sir."

"Do you realize that your men and you are dirty and unshaven? Even your helicopter is dirty."

"Sorry, major, but we've been doing a lot of flying, and we haven't had time."

"When you allow military discipline to break down, morale breaks down and units cease to function as military units."

A lecture—I was getting a fucking lecture about military preparedness from a fucking major who obviously had no job and did not realize there was a fucking war going on all around him.

"As I said, major, we have been busy."

"*Busy*? You're not busy now. You're eating aren't you?"

Snick. I turned to see that the crew chief had unlatched his M-60 machine gun. He was pointing it directly at the major. "Shall I shoot him, sir?"

No one moved.

The major stood still, looking between the crew chief and me. His eyes were wide in disbelief. I looked at the jungle about one hundred yards away. A body dumped ten feet past the tree line would disappear forever, and no one would even look up at the sound of a single shot.

"No," I said. "No ... don't shoot."

The crew chief kept the M-60 aimed at the major. After a moment, the major took a single step backward, turned to his left, and walked rapidly away. No one said a word. The crew chief lowered his weapon, and we all continued eating our C-Rations.

24
Tet

War is a series of catastrophes that results in a victory.

~Georges Clemenceau

January 30, 1968—Phu Loi, South Vietnam

"Try this," Frank said, handing me a rocks glass half-filled with an amber liquid.

"What's this?"

"Have you ever tried Rémy Martin?"

"No," I said. "What's that?"

"It's a cognac," he replied.

"Okay. What's a cognac?"

"It's wine that's been distilled."

"Oo-kaay? Let me try it."

"This is VSOP, which means Very Special Old Preserve or something like that. Anyway, it means that it has been aged, and in the case of Rémy it is very smooth."

Holding the glass up to the light I swirled the amber liquid noting the richness of the color. Sniffing it I found it had a very pleasant aroma. Sounds of gunfire echoing from the base perimeter served as a rather surreal backdrop as I took a sip and began a life-long love affair with Rémy Martin Cognac.

Grounded three days for having logged more than 120 hours of flight time in the preceding thirty days, I had caught a flight back to Phu Loi to visit with my friend Frank Belsky. An attack that evening on Phu Loi required the services of nearly every pilot. Scheduled for an early morning mission, Frank was exempt from duties that evening.

Although rumors had been floating around for a couple of weeks that attacks would coincide with Tet—one rumor had the psychic Jeane Dixon prophesying there would be a bloodbath—none of us realized this was the beginning of a series of coordinated attacks all over South Vietnam. U.S. history would call this the Tet Offensive, and although it would be a significant military failure for the North Vietnamese, the images of the battles, which were broadcast on the evening news, would eventually turn American public opinion strongly against the war.

Frank and I were the only two occupants of the officers' club. Even the bartender was out on the line. We sat there, drinking the cognac, talking until late at night, and enjoying being the only two people who were not presently involved in the fighting. We did not pay too much attention to what we considered just another battle raging out on the perimeter.

At some point in the evening, another pilot came in for a quick drink.

"How's it going out there?" asked Frank.

"There's all kinds of shit going on all over the country. VC are attacking everywhere. Saigon and Bien Hoa are under attack."

"Bien Hoa?" I said.

"Yeah," said the pilot. "I heard they overran the perimeter on the Air Force side."

"Well, shit," I said. "Guess I should go back. Frank, can I get a ride sometime tomorrow?"

"Yeah. I'll take you. We'll head out a couple minutes early."

The sun had yet to make an appearance when Frank dropped me off at the 101st helipad. The military had different plans for each of us, and it would be three years before I saw him again.

At approximately 0830 hours on the morning of January 31, helicopters from A Company, 101st Aviation Battalion, 101st Airborne Division gained the distinction of making the first airborne combat assault on an American Embassy. The embassy in Saigon had come under attack during the night trapping Marine and embassy personnel inside. Our company helicopters, led by Warrant Officer Milo Overstreet, landed on the helipad located on the roof of the embassy and discharged soldiers who organized an assault on the enemy troops around the building. Years later, that same helipad would become infamous during the final evacuation of Saigon.

That evening the enemy mounted another attack on Bien Hoa. It was visible from our barracks, and those of us who were not flying watched the war, many finding front-row seats on the roof of our hootch. With their attached million-candle-power flares having burned out, ghostly parachutes drifted over our area. Some pilot commented that it would be neat to hang one over his army cot. This resulted in several men rushing to capture one.

Flying a patrol over Bien Hoa the next evening, I watched tracer rounds flick out from unseen positions, clearly defining the overlapping fields of fire that American troops had laid out. Occasionally, returned fire followed. We radioed it in; although, I am reasonably certain that the troops on the receiving end were clearly aware of the source.

25
Beer Run

We are here to drink beer. We are here to kill war. We are here to laugh at the odds and live our lives so well that Death will tremble to take us.

~CHARLES BUKOWSKI

Early February, 1968—Bien Hoa, South Vietnam

A lull in the fighting a couple of days later gave us the opportunity to attend to less serious matters. We decided to rectify a minor crisis: our dangerously low beer supply needed replenishing. A group of us decided to make a run to the Air Force PX located on the other side of the Bien Hoa runway. We had three options. One involved going west around the runway. The advantage was that we would remain inside U.S.-held territory for the entire trip. The disadvantage was that it was a long trip. The second option meant going around the east end of the runway.

The advantage with this option was that it would be a shortened trip. The disadvantage was that for a relatively short distance we would be outside of the perimeter and the safety that it provided. We never considered the third option of not going.

After discussing the pros and cons, we all reasoned that with the fighting over, we could safely make the shorter trip. After a brief discussion about whether we should take our combat gear (helmets, weapons, flak jackets), we decided that we should; the MPs at the Air Force gate might not let us in without it.

Obtaining a three-quarter-ton truck and loading everyone aboard, including pilots Morgan, Narburgh, Neal, Mays, and some of the enlisted crewmembers and maintenance personnel, we began our mission during yet another dreary, cool day. The bodies of Viet Cong and NVA littered the terrain. One body, caught and held upright by a fence, still appeared to be running toward the base. His family would never know his fate. They would only know that he never returned home.

Passing through the gate and onto the perimeter road, we began the short stretch, less than one mile, to the Air Force gate. Built above the surrounding terrain to keep it from flooding during the rainy season, the road made anything on it an easy target. The swampy-looking land on each side of the road would probably have been rice paddies if the Bien Hoa airfield had not been there. I sat facing east, not paying attention to my surroundings as I tried to think of things that I needed to purchase at the PX.

One of the maintenance staff sergeants sitting across from me jumped up, whipped his M-16 into firing position, and yelled, "I see them. I see them!"

Whom did he see? As best I could in the crowded truck, I turned to see men running across the open area behind me. Turning back toward the east, I was startled to see little splashes of water and mud as bullets impacted in the swampy ground. I could hear them whine through the air when they ricocheted off a wire fence that stood about twenty feet from the road. Next, the MPs staffing the Air Force gate opened fire, and we all realized we were in the middle of a deadly crossfire.

A truck in front of us stopped forcing us to halt. Men jumped from the truck and slid down the side of the road for protection. I jumped out of the back of our truck, squatted down, and stopped—not the best move, as the next guy out landed on my head. I scurried over to the relative safety of the sloping side of the road.

Lying in the dirt I pulled out my Smith & Wesson .38 Special, the standard pistol issued to 101st pilots. Looking at it, I realized that it was a worthless weapon in a combat zone. In addition, it was not loaded. After a frenzied and clumsy attempt to get the bullets from my pocket and into the pistol, I vowed to keep it loaded until I left Vietnam. Worthless or not, it felt good to have something in my hand. An M-16 would have felt much better.

I then rolled over onto my belly and peered over the top of the road. A movie scene stretched out before me. Men ran firing their guns. Americans returned fire and men fell. I saw bullets striking the wall by the Air Force gate. I was in a full adrenalin rush, and I wanted to join in the fighting.

"Mr. Bercaw, get your head down!" This came from the same staff sergeant who had first spotted the enemy.

Reluctantly I slid back down until my head was below the level of the road. I really wanted to watch.

Helicopter blades beating the air sounded from the north. We all looked to see the narrow silhouettes of two Cobra gunships reminding me of fish sliding through water. New to the Army inventory they were the first Cobras I had seen. We all stuck our heads above the edge to watch as the first one rolled in and opened up with mini-guns, producing a loud burping sound as approximately 4,000 rounds per minute spewed down upon the hapless enemy troops out in the open. The second Cobra rolled in and rockets screamed down, exploding among the enemy and sending white-hot pieces of shrapnel whizzing in all directions. The noises alone were beyond frightening. I felt reluctant sympathy for the men who were running across the field knowing that death was a certainty.

For the first time uneasiness settled over me. My skin seemed to shrink and it felt tight around my body. Glancing at my forearm, I saw all of the hairs standing on end. Could the gunship pilots tell that we were Americans, or were we just more targets from their lofty perch high above the battlefield? It would not take more than a twitch by an adrenalin-fueled pilot to ruin our day. We just wanted some beer.

Just then, a large tanker truck loaded with jet fuel pulled up. With its air brakes hissing, it stopped behind our truck. Jim Morgan crawled up the side of the road and ran toward the driver yelling for him to back his truck away from our position.

"I can't turn around!" the driver yelled back.

"Just back up. Don't try to turn around," Jim yelled, pointing in the direction of our gate.

The driver hesitated.

"Back it up. Just fucking back it up," Jim yelled, still pointing while advancing on the driver. Finally, the driver put the truck into reverse and began to back slowly down the road.

Jim sprinted for our truck, hopped in, and turned it around. He leaned over and yelled out the passenger window, "Get on the truck. Get on the truck!"

We all scrambled aboard and within a couple of minutes, we were back within the relative safety of our gate. After a few moments of consultation, we decided to go around the west end of the runway to the PX. Strangely, I felt a sense of disappointment. It had been exhilarating out there, and it was now over. I had wanted to stay for just a bit longer.

What had prompted the enemy to make a daylight infantry attack across a large open area against withering American firepower? It was essentially a suicide mission on a non-newsworthy target. The attack was too small-scale to be of any propaganda value, and it had virtually no chance of succeeding. Am I wrong to believe that some military commander just threw away the lives of some very brave soldiers? Forty-five years later, I am more sympathetic to those lives than I was then.

26
North Along the Coast

Duty is the most sublime word in our language. Do your duty in all things. You cannot do more. You should never wish to do less.

~General Robert E. Lee

February, 1968—Bien Hoa, South Vietnam

The operations officer stuck his head inside the door, "Overstreet, you and Bercaw take two aircraft north to Quang Tri (*kwang tree*) tomorrow morning. You'll be supporting elements of the first brigade."

"Quang Tri?" I said. "Where the hell is that?"

"It's just about as far north as you can go without entering North Vietnam," Milo said.

"That's about correct," the operations officer continued. "Take enough gear for a week."

I was glad to be going with Milo. He had more time in Vietnam than I had, having flown with the 1st Cav before coming to the 101st. Short, pugnacious, and having a reputation as a good pilot, he exuded an air of competence that made me feel more confident. My copilot was Warrant Officer Neal whom I barely knew. As instructed, I took a week's worth of clothing and personal items. However, we never returned to Bien Hoa, and six months would pass before I saw my gear again.

This was the rainy season. The usual overcast skies held us to an altitude of about one-thousand feet most of the way up the coast—high enough for a nice view, but low enough to be dangerous. Having been as far south as the resort area of Vung Tau, I now saw the length of South Vietnam as we flew north. I began to appreciate that Vietnam was a remarkably varied country. Rice paddies dominated the Delta. Jungles began to control the terrain north of Saigon, and hills that eventually turned into mountains were the norm beginning somewhere north of Song Be. The landscape leveled out along the coast around Hue (*way*) up to the DMZ.

After a stop at Da Nang, where we refueled both aircraft and crew, we continued our journey north. As we flew through the pass north of Da Nang, a vista of mountains greeted us. They descended right to the edge of a beach that disappeared from sight far to the north. Neither for the first time nor for the last, I wished I could call a timeout and stop off to enjoy the beautiful country along the way.

The stretch of terrain between Da Nang and Phu Bai (*foo bye*) seemed to us to be a perfect place for an ambush given the close proximity of the mountains to the ocean. To avoid ground fire we flew out over the ocean, but we stayed close enough to the beach that we could make it back in the event of an engine failure. In the days to come this stretch of

Vietnam would become rather treacherous. The cloud cover would sometimes force us to fly so low that we would literally be skimming the tops of the waves. We would see every type of military aircraft down there with us. It kept us alert.

While refueling at Phu Bai, we received a briefing. We had heard no real news for days. We finally departed mid-afternoon staying below fifty feet as we headed out on the final leg of our journey. Skirting Hue to the west along the Perfume River, our intent was to connect with Highway 1—Bernard Fall's *Street Without Joy*[13]—and follow that to Quang Tri. I tagged along about one-half mile behind Milo.

The sun peeked intermittently through the clouds. This lifted our spirits as we zoomed along, anticipating hot meals and some rest. I refrained from dropping down and zipping along just above the surface of the river because of the possibility of wires strung over it. We spied uniformed troops ahead of us, marching along Highway 1 and heading in the direction of Hue. Since they were marching and not riding, I assumed they were ARVN troops and not U.S. soldiers.

Milo's aircraft flew over the top of them and then made a steep turn—so steep that I was looking at the top of his helicopter. I assumed that he was showing off, as pilots love to do. I expected him to continue up the highway.

However, he continued his turn until he was heading back in the direction of Phu Bai, and then he passed me.

"Milo, what's going on?"

"We just got the shit shot out of us."

Surprised and confused, I resisted the urge to fly over the top of the marching troops, and I turned back to follow Milo.

---

13 Fall, Bernard, *Street Without Joy: The French Debacle In Indochina*, Stackpole Military History Series, originally published in 1961.

Once on the ground, Milo explained, "Those motherfuckers dropped to one knee and opened fire on us as we flew over."

"Who?" I asked. "The troops?"

"Yeah. I think they were fucking NVA. In fucking uniform. Walking down the middle of the fucking road."

Milo was upset.

It was soon determined that his aircraft would require repairs before we could continue our trip north. We found the captain who had given us the briefing earlier to see if we could mooch some maintenance and parts from them. We explained what had happened.

"Oh, yeah," he said. "There's still a lot of fighting up there."

I filed this in my no-shit folder and wondered why it had not crossed his mind to include this information in our initial briefing.

Arriving at the Marine base in Quang Tri late in the afternoon a couple of days later, the Marines allowed us to park our Hueys on their ramp. However, they would not let us stay the night inside the perimeter. We set up camp immediately outside of the wire. We had a few letters to mail, but the Marines would not accept them.[14]

The next couple of months were rather unique. The 101st sent a handful of helicopters to join us. Everyone was desperate for our services, and we could more or less pick and choose the missions that we accepted. The weather was terrible, and on many days we flew in conditions that did not conform to any regulation in any book. Essentially, if we could bring the helicopter to a hover and we could still see,

---

14 I never discovered the reasoning behind the refusals, but forty-five years later, it still pisses me off.

we would fly. I cannot remember a single day that we did not fly.

As a result, we flew many support missions for the Marines. Their pilots, saddled with some engraved-in-stone regulations about when they could and could not fly, spent much of this period grounded. The Army had similar regulations, but like many rules, obeying them would have been an easy—and legal—way to shirk our duties.[15] We flew.

We ran supply missions for the Marines, medevaced their wounded, and transported troops for them. The most dangerous mission that I flew in Vietnam was a mission to extract a young Marine stranded in the mountains just north of Da Nang—within eyesight of the big Marine airbase located there. We gave the Marines C-Rations from our own supply, as many of them had not received any support for days. Eventually, the Marines in the field began coming directly to us with requests for missions, certain that their own command would ignore or reject them.

One miserable day, as we landed by the temporary medical center that had been set up in the ballpark at Phu Bai, a young Marine lieutenant, angry and frustrated nearly to tears, ran up and literally begged us to take a mission for him. Marine helicopters sat tied down not fifty yards away from us. To the best of my knowledge, the Marine Corps never officially acknowledged any of the missions that we flew for them or the supplies that we gave them.

---

15 Guidelines and not rules, I believe, should govern combat operations. Rules are inflexible, and in wartime they tend to get people killed.

27
The DMZ

Danger and delight grow on one stalk.

~SCOTTISH PROVERB

February, 1968—The Demilitarized Zone between North Vietnam and South Vietnam

Departing Quang Tri for what turned out to be the last time, I asked my copilot if he would like to see the DMZ, which was located a short distance north. Actually, I did not care what he wanted, as I had already headed in that direction.

A high, thick overcast painted the flat landscape with a drab gray light. An endless drizzle made the short sparse vegetation look damp and dismal. There were no roads, no buildings, no trees, and no people. Had God *and* man rejected this land? As we continued north, I began to feel very alone and vulnerable. Was it possible that men had ever walked across this plain?

My anxiety increased as we continued moving farther from any immediate assistance that we might need. To die anywhere on this prairie would be to die alone and forgotten. The area appeared unworthy of any death—the enemy's or ours—and the weight of such futility seemed to make even the vegetation reluctant to grow. Could even sunlight make this place pleasant?

When I eventually decided that we were near or at the DMZ, I became even more vigilant. Who might be observing us—two foolish helicopter pilots out on a lark?

I continued my flight until I was certain that we had crossed the southern line of the DMZ—just to say that I had done it. Then I made a quick turn and fled back to the dubious safety of South Vietnam.

28
Medevac

Do what you can, with what you have, where you are.

~Theodore Roosevelt

Early March, 1968—Vicinity of the Hai Van (*hi van*) Pass, north of Da Nang, South Vietnam

Mountains marching out to sea form the northern protective barrier of the Da Nang harbor. The mountains continue easterly for three or four miles from the Hai Van Pass. Then they end abruptly. Another small mountain peak forms an island slightly less than one-half mile east. These mountains, usually shrouded in clouds while I was operating in the area, forced us to fly out over the ocean and cut through the pass between the island and the rest of the mountains.

One day, when Neal and I flew down from Phu Bai, the Da Nang tower controller asked if we would call a platoon that was located somewhere in the mountains to the north.

They had requested an emergency medevac of one of their members. Agreeing to this, we turned back and established their location in a little saddleback that was about a mile or less from the point where the mountains met the sea. The injured man, we learned, was a Marine.

Approaching their position from the south presented us with a host of problems—mainly they were socked-in weather-wise. A headwind roaring over the mountain gave us a very slow groundspeed as we approached. That was good. Slowing the Huey to about fifty knots, we looked for any sign of the unit or even the ground. Carried along by the headwind, a rapidly moving cloud layer hugged the mountaintop. This was bad. Another layer of clouds sat over the mountain like a cap. Trying to move up between these layers proved to be disorienting. Making a sharp turn using the cyclic and the pedals, I dove back down the mountain until I was clear of the clouds. I attempted this two or three times with no success. Meanwhile, Neal engaged the radio operator in conversation to determine their exact location using the FM Homing device and to see if the operator could give us some guidance based on the noise that our helicopter was creating. Finally giving up on approaching from the south, I flew around the pass to look at the situation from the north side of the mountains.

Clouds moved up the side from near the base and then over the top, clinging to the mountain all the way. The cap of clouds was still there, but it sat a little higher on this side. Flying close to the opening between layers, I again found myself disoriented.

Reluctantly we decided that we could not complete the mission, and I headed back around the pass for Da Nang. When we called the radio operator and informed him of our decision, he informed us that the Marine had been on the ground wounded for twenty-four hours.

"Twenty-four hours?" Neal said. "Why haven't the Marines come out to pick him up?"

The Marine's Marble Mountain aviation facility was within eyesight. It was about twelve miles away.

"How bad is this guy?" I asked the radio operator.

"He's bad."

"Okay. Let's go take another look at it," I said to the crew. "Maybe things have improved. If anyone sees any sight of the ground – be it below us or above us – let me know immediately, and give me specifics as to where it is in relation to the aircraft, okay?"

I received a chorus of affirmations.

Once again, we approached the site from the south, and once again, we had to turn back due to lost visibility. We were all on edge about the mountains. The maps our operations issued to us when we had moved north were one-over-the-world.[16] They did not provide detailed information about the area. None of us was certain how high the peaks were that surrounded us.

After circling out over the bay a couple of times, I asked the crew, "Do you want to take a look at the backside again?"

Again, I got a chorus of affirmations.

Reaching the north side for the second time, I analyzed the situation as best I could. The wind rushed over the mountain, but it stayed close to the mountain itself. Otherwise, it would have blown the cap of clouds away, or so I reasoned. I also noted that the clouds climbing the mountain were not

---

16 We called the 1:250,000 scale maps one-over-the-world maps. More suited to high-flying, fast-moving aircraft, they were of minimal use to helicopter pilots. We normally carried 1:50,000 scale maps – the same type that the infantry carried.

as thick as they were on the south side, and we were able to catch momentary glimpses of the ground. Maybe, just maybe, we would be able to spot the unit.

"Okay. Here's the plan: we're going to approach from this side to see what we can see. If we lose sight of the ground but I maintain this heading, we should be okay, as long as we climb like a bat out of hell." It seemed to me that as long as I followed the rapidly moving clouds, we would stay between the peaks. "We can contact the tower for help. What I want from you is the same kind of information that I asked for before, okay?"

Again, I received affirmations, only they were less enthusiastic than before.

I called the unit on the mountain and said, "Do you have any of those big million-candle-power flares available? If so, can you pop it right where you want us to land?"

The unit confirmed that they had these flares.

"Let me know when it's lit."

After a lengthy pause, during which we orbited out over the ocean, the unit called, "It's lit."

"Okay, here we go," I said. "Everyone, stay alert."

I approached the mountain as slowly as I could, and I tried to stay above the clouds that were rushing by below us. We quickly got between them and the cloud cap, and this meant that we were committed. There would be no turning back. My pucker factor increased accordingly. The crew chimed in with comments, expressing a good deal of doubt about what we were doing. I refrained from saying that it was too late to worry about that.

We continued to move forward at about twenty-five knots. With the exception of an occasional peek at the ground through fleeting breaks in the cloud cover rushing by a few feet below us, and a shattered tree stump here and there, everything was white and featureless. I began to question the wisdom of my decision to attempt this medevac.

"We're going to get ourselves killed in here." someone said.

"Listen to me. We *are* going to get killed, if you don't start giving me the information I asked for."

This caused everyone to start babbling at once.

"Stop. Just say whatever you have to say one time, then be quiet until you have something new to tell me."

This seemed to calm everyone down a little bit.

"I see the flare. I see the flare," someone, probably my gunner, shouted.

It appeared to our right front, burning brightly through the lower layer of clouds. I maneuvered in that direction and gradually descended. We did not have far to descend. At most, we were only fifty feet above the ground.

"Keep an eye out for the landing spot."

I found myself with few features I could use for orientation. Descending into the moving cloud deck, a vicious tail wind hit us. Fear of disorientation made me resist turning into the wind, and I did not want to exit the area to the north. Exiting to the north would require that we avoid numerous obstacles when we departed. However, the south side was wide open, and we would be over the bay once we were clear of the mountains.

I fixated on a couple of shattered tree stumps that were near enough that I could see them through the rushing clouds. I was afraid to take my eyes off them long enough to look around for the bright flare. I was not going to find the landing area unless I blundered on to it.

"Guide me to the landing area," I said.

Neal and the gunner gave me directions that moved us forward and to the right. Once over the area, Neal called for descent.

"Stop," the gunner said. "You're about to hit some stumps with the tail rotor."

"Can I move left or right to avoid them?"

"No. The damned things are all over the place. Don't go any lower."

"Okay," I said. "Can they load the wounded guy onboard at this height?"

"Yeah. It should be okay."

"Neal, put me on the tower's frequency."

Reaching across the console, he switched me to the VHF radio. "You're up."

"Da Nang Tower, this is Army helicopter One-One-Eight. I'm on top of the mountain about ten miles north squawking twelve hundred. Can you see me?"

"This is Da Nang Tower, negative on that. I do not have you on the radar."

"Okay, Tower. I'm about to depart this location, heading south. When you spot me, will you tell me when I am clear of the mountains so that I can let down out of the overcast?"

"One-One-Eight, I am unable to give you any information on the mountains."

I started to develop a very negative opinion about the efficiency of everyone in the Da Nang area. The Huey began to wobble as the wounded man was loaded onboard, adding to my workload and level of stress.

"Okay, can you tell me if you have anyone flying around in this area who might be traffic for me when I depart this location?"

"One-One-Eight, there are numerous targets all over the area. I have no information about them."

My negative opinion grew even more negative.

The wobbling of the helicopter stopped. "We're up," the gunner said.

"Okay," I said. "Here we go. Give me the same information I've asked for all along. We're going to climb straight ahead for about two minutes and then let down until we break out."

With that, I pulled in a good amount of power and headed for the safety, I hoped, of the Da Nang harbor.

About thirty seconds later, the Da Nang tower operator said, "One-One-Eight, ident."

Neal triggered the identification feature of the transponder.

"One-One-Eight, you are in radar contact. Turn to heading one-seven-five degrees for Da Nang."

I was relieved that the tower operator could see us, and I really hoped that this meant we were clear of the mountains.

"Roger, one-seven-five degrees."

About a minute later, we commenced our descent and broke out of the clouds around one thousand feet. I called for clearance to the medevac pad.

"Sir," the gunner said, "this guy says we can just drop him off anywhere, and he'll walk."

"Walk?"

"Yes, sir. And to be honest, this guy doesn't look wounded. I'm betting he just wanted off the mountain to catch an R and R flight or something like that."

I canceled the request for the medevac pad and requested to land near the terminal. Upon landing, the Marine jumped off, turned around, waved, and walked away. We all sat there dumbstruck.

"Did we just risk our lives for someone who's not hurt?" Neal asked.

As we hovered out for departure, we passed by a civilian passenger jet that was sitting on the taxiway. Two stewardesses standing in the doorway waved to us. I turned the

Huey so that we were facing them and hovered sideways. One of the women raised her skirt to show us her legs. I gave a little bow with the helicopter, turned, and headed back north to the war. I still remember her legs.

29
Thirty Seconds

Danger – if you meet it promptly and without flinching – you will reduce the danger by half. Never run away from anything. Never!

~**Sir Winston Churchill**

1968—Somewhere in South Vietnam

Briefly distracted by the tall elephant grass rushing past one hundred feet below, I carelessly dropped down into the turbulence created by the helicopter in front of me, and the Huey began to buck and shake. After pulling in additional power, the aircraft struggled but managed to climb high enough to put the rotor system back into clean air thereby sparing me the sarcasm of all the pilots to the rear.

All of the helicopters were slowly rising and falling relative to each other reminding me of a merry-go-round at the county fair. However, it was a dangerous merry-go-round as the separation between helicopters was only about twenty feet—less than the length of a rotor blade. The tail rotor of the aircraft in front of me—a giant buzz saw—looked ready to cut me in half if I got any closer.

Like a river rushing toward a waterfall, we descended into a valley speeding along ever closer to the ground. The *whomp, whomp, whomp* of the rotor blades, amplified by the twenty helicopters in our two formations, certainly sounded like approaching thunder to anyone on the ground. The Viet Cong called the sound Muttering Death.

Obscured under a cloud of smoke and dust from an artillery barrage, the landing zone was about three miles in front of me. The intent was not so much to kill anyone but to make them keep their heads down long enough for us to land, unload the troops, and then get the hell out of Dodge. I hoped that the coordination was good between the artillery and the flight leader of the first formation, because aborting the landing and climbing their heavily-laden Hueys out of the narrow valley would be difficult.

The radios came alive with chatter. Troops issued last-minute orders over the FM radios, the gunships coordinated with one another on the UHF radios, and all of this competed with the two Huey formations that were communicating over the VHF radios.

"Get on the controls with me," I instructed my copilot, a new kid whose name I could not remember.

I felt him clumsily placing his hands and feet on the controls.

"Don't actually touch the controls," I said, "just stay near them. That way you can take over quicker if I'm hit."

I could sense him looking at me. The reality of the situation we were rapidly approaching had begun to register. I knew he was scared. *Tough shit. We've all gone through this.*

"White smoke. I have white smoke," someone called, indicating that he had spotted the last round that the artillery had fired.

Whump! *Whump*! *Whump*! I nearly jumped out of my seat as the gunships started walking rockets in beside us. Each explosion, which I saw with my peripheral vision, came so close that I wondered if we were taking shrapnel hits. My adrenalin rush went into overdrive.

"Sir, can we open fire?" the door gunner yelled over the intercom.

"Door gunner, watch for the gunships and open fire. Chief," I said to the crew chief on the other side of the helicopter, "do *not* fire. We're too close to the other aircraft."

"Yes, sir," the crew chief said, obviously pissed off that he could not join in the general mayhem.

The door gunner opened fire, and I felt as though someone was standing behind me hitting me on both sides of my head. The noise was deafening and painful. Speech over the intercom was nearly impossible.

"C and C ship over the ridgeline; you have antiaircraft fire walking up behind you." This anonymous call came over one of the emergency frequencies.

Risking a quick look up, I spotted three dark clouds from explosions right behind the mission commander's aircraft high above the ridgeline. The pilot had obviously heard the call because the Huey nosed over and dove for the relative safety of low-level flight.

"White flight is out." The first flight was departing the landing zone.

Our formation, Red flight, began deceleration in preparation for landing. The helicopter wobbled slightly as the troops in the back shifted positions to the doors of the aircraft. All the while, they were yelling to one another, psyching themselves up for the assault. Watching the other helicopters for changes in attitude, I glanced ahead to get a close look at the landing area prior to touchdown.

Thirty seconds, thirty seconds. All I had to do was survive the next thirty seconds.

My adrenaline-fueled brain felt wonderfully alert, noting and analyzing everything developing around me. Dying because I failed to notice some crucial detail was not an option.

Now shouting, grunting, and sounding like animals, the troops prepared to jump into whatever hell awaited them on the ground. I jumped when mud thrown up by one of the gunships' exploding rockets splattered the windshield.

"Gunner, you okay back there?"

No response. He had probably never heard the question over the noise and his own adrenalin rush, but he continued to fire his weapon.

Thirty seconds. Thirty seconds.

The individual Hueys began to move about as each pilot jockeyed for a clear area to put his helicopter down.

"Gunner, cease fire. Cease fire. Troops on the ground." My microphone amplified the sounds of his gunfire and increased the pain in my ears to the point I wondered if I would lose my hearing.

Approximately twenty-five feet above the ground, I pulled the nose of my Huey up into a high flare, thus rapidly reducing my airspeed. Fifteen feet. The troops shouting in the back nearly overwhelmed my ability to hear the radios. The grass, now flattened from the rotor wash, revealed a few obstacles that I would need to avoid. Five feet. The helicopter wobbled from side-to-side as the troops began jumping from the aircraft. We were now a large, slow target, and the soldiers wanted to get away from us as quickly as possible.

Crunch! The heels of the skids hit the ground hard. I expected to roll forward onto the toes of the skids and take off again.

We just sat there.

"Chalk Two is taking fire."

I looked forward, trying to spot the second aircraft, but I could not see anything happening.

"This is Lead, roger," Chalk One responded. "Got a problem. Hang on."

"Chalk Ten is taking fire."

"Chalk Nine is taking fire ... taking hits."

It was peaceful near the middle of the formation where I sat looking out my door at a large field of tall grasses bordered by an undulating tree line that was about one hundred yards away. A warm breeze carried the scent of the fresh earth, blasted into the air by the artillery barrage, through the cabin commingled with the smells of burnt jet fuel and the residue from the explosions. The troops who were lying on the ground rolled over onto their backs and looked back at us. They wanted us to depart.

"Lead, this is Chalk Ten. Get a move on."

No response.

Two aircraft came from behind and passed on our right side. Chalk Nine and Chalk Ten had broken out of formation and were leaving the area.

"Lead." someone yelled. "If you can respond, do so; otherwise, Chalk Two, take the lead."

Looking forward I could see Chalk One begin lifting off, and I began raising the collective lever to increase the power. The total time on the ground had been about a minute—a very long minute. During the climb to altitude, we began a slow left turn to return to the pickup zone for another load of troops.

"Nice landing," the copilot said. I detected sarcasm.

"Hey, we're still alive. You have the controls."

"I have the controls."

With my muscles relaxing, I sat back and looked about. Below us, the jungle, a beautiful mélange of greens, led us away from the problems that were now facing the men we had left behind. The sky, painted a crisp clear blue mixed with luminous billowing clouds, promised peace and safety. The air—oh, so sweet—filled my lungs. The formation stretched out before me moving from sun to shade in a long, lazy turn. In that moment, I loved my helicopter. I loved my fellow pilots and crewmembers. In that moment, I did not wish to be anywhere on earth except in the seat of my helicopter. Life was very good.

30
Propriety

de·co·rum: dignified propriety of behavior, speech, dress, etc.

~DICTIONARY.COM

Early 1968—Phu Bai, South Vietnam

Trudging through ankle-deep mud, I was not happy. It was early. I was tired. The weather was bad, and I had nothing to look forward to except for another long and dangerous day. I cleaned my boots off as best I could before getting into the helicopter. Settling in, I stowed my steel-pot helmet under my seat and moved my cowboy holster with my Smith & Wesson .38 Special pistol around so it hung down in front of me, providing some dubious protection for my crotch. I placed my map between the seat and the center console, adjusted my chicken plate, fastened my harness, and lowered my seat as low as it could go with the helmet underneath, hoping to make myself a more difficult target. Conferring with the copilot and crew about the first mission, I reached for my flight helmet, which was hanging just behind me to my right. It was not there.

"Goddamn," I shouted. "Son of a bitch!"

"What?" my copilot asked.

"I forgot my fucking flight helmet!"

"I'll get it, sir," the crew chief said.

"No, it's my goddamned fault. I'll go get the goddamned thing."

Off I stomped, splattering mud and swearing all the way there and all the way back. This time, I did not take as much care cleaning my boots before crawling up to get into my seat. Looking into the back of the aircraft, I saw that we had passengers, something I had not noticed the first time. I spotted the Christian cross on the collar of a young captain. *Great. Just fucking great.* I had a chaplain onboard!

"Good morning, sir," I said. "Sorry about the outburst."

He just smiled at me. We dropped him off at our first stop.

"Why didn't someone tell me he was onboard?" I asked.

Laughter was my answer.

The next morning I again found myself trudging through the ankle-deep mud. Again, I was tired and again, I had nothing but more bad weather and danger waiting for me. Arriving at the aircraft, I looked in the back and saw passengers, including the same chaplain.

"Good morning, sir."

"Good morning, Mr. Bercaw." He smiled. "I trust you remembered your helmet today."

31
Defining Moment

Courage is doing what you're afraid to do. There can be no courage unless you're scared.

~EDWARD VERNON RICKENBACKER

Early 1968—The mountains of Vietnam south of Hue, South Vietnam

The major seated in the back of my helicopter had grown impatient with the progress that his people had made on the ground. "Charlie One-Niner, this is Alpha Six. I need you to speed it up, and I need to know what is going on down there. Over."

Unseen in the thick jungle below, his lieutenant whispered on the radio, "The only thing I know is that I want to get off this fucking mountain."

It was a very reasonable request. I did not even want to be flying above it. I continued to orbit, dreading any calls for an emergency medevac for wounded and dying American soldiers should the enemy discover them. Given the terrain below us—low mountains covered with heavy jungle—any rescue attempt would involve some tricky and dangerous flying. A call came over the radio interrupting these thoughts.

"Eagle One-One-Five, change to your company push. Over."

Upon changing to my company frequency, the operations officer instructed me to call a unit that was reportedly in contact with an enemy force. After receiving a general location of the action, I again changed frequencies and heard men yelling orders. Other men were screaming for immediate assistance. The background sounds of automatic weapons and explosions accompanied all of the radio transmissions. My stomach knotted as adrenalin surged through my body.

At the first opportunity, I placed a call over the radio to the commander on the ground. "Bravo Six, this is Eagle One-One-Five. We are a U-H-One-H helicopter just a few miles north of you waiting for your instructions."

"One-One-Five, this is Bravo Six. We're in contact with a company-size force. We've got dead and wounded and need an emergency medevac." My pulse rate increased a bit more.

"Ah, roger, Bravo Six," I responded. "We're on our way. Put the most seriously wounded on the first load and the rest on the next. We'll get the dead when we can. Over."

"This is Six, roger."

"And Six, this is One-One-Five, also request that you set up a perimeter for us."

"This is Six. Negative on that request—unable to comply."

"Roger."

Due to the situation on the ground, I had not really expected them to comply. However, anytime I landed in an unsecured area, I always requested that the force on the ground give me a perimeter. Sometimes they did; sometimes they did not. I was never certain what protection it would give me, but it made me feel better.

The FM homing device gave me the general direction of the radio transmissions, and I turned southeast toward the battle. Nosing the Huey over the edge of the mountain we quickly hit the airspeed red line, and the Huey bucked and rattled. The major in the back was pissed off that we were taking him away from his men. I could not blame him.

Uncertain of the exact location I called for smoke. Two plumes appeared—one purple and one yellow. I correctly identified the color purple as belonging to Bravo Six. Apparently, the enemy was monitoring the frequency and had popped a captured smoke grenade hoping to draw us to that location. A couple minutes later the last of the purple smoke drifted away, and we were still about five miles out. Losing track of the location I called for another smoke.

Glancing back at my crew I noted that the door gunner had his gun up in the ready position. "Listen up, back there. Do *not* fire. Don't even return fire! We have no idea where our guys are."

A large automatic weapon began firing at us as we approached the site. Its throaty *boom, boom, boom* seemed to bounce and echo around the inside of the Huey. My heart kicked into overdrive, my neck began to hurt from my hammering pulse, and my ever-present dull headache became a sharp pain behind my right eye. I had to open my mouth to gain a full breath.

The enemy kept firing, and I kept the airspeed high—until the last possible minute when I yanked the Huey's nose back into an extreme flare to reduce the airspeed for the landing. The copilot immediately yelled, "High RPM. High RPM."

Creating a huge cloud of dust, I quickly lost sight of the ground. Angry for not having anticipated it, all I could do was hope that I had judged everything correctly. We touched down without as much as a bounce. I silently congratulated myself.

Apparitions that looked vaguely like U.S. soldiers moved rapidly toward us out of the swirling dust and smoke. It was a visual cacophony of dirty and fearful faces, blood, and mangled bodies. The air, rancid from gun smoke and the stench of unwashed bodies, caught in my throat causing me to cough. The continuing sounds of the battle, close and ominous, added a heightened sense of immediacy to the chaotic scene. My pulse pounded painfully in my ears.

"Give me an up, chief," I said unnecessarily to the crew chief, who was standing about five feet from the aircraft connected by a long communications cord, directing the loading of wounded men.

I sat there, as I always did in these circumstances, willing myself to stay put until the crew chief gave me the signal that we were ready to depart. I kept my left arm locked straight so that I would not inadvertently start to pull in the power before we were ready. I listened for the unmistakable sounds of bullets slamming into the aircraft, and I tried to imagine what it would feel like to have a round smash through the aluminum and into my body. It seemed that we had been on the ground for a long time and the troops were just milling around even though I knew that we had only been there for seconds and everyone was working as fast as humanly possible.

As I sat there watching the controlled pandemonium around me, two soldiers carrying a stretcher ran up beside my door. They paused for a moment waiting for their turn to place the wounded soldier onto the aircraft. I looked down at this man—a boy, actually—noting his uniform covered in dirt and dark red blood. His eyes, trapped in a face that was pale and yellowish from shock, looked at me for a moment. Then he did something astonishing: lying there amongst all the havoc around us, he smiled.

Surprised by this ordinary gesture in an extraordinary situation, I smiled back, and then comprehension flowed over me like a wave. He smiled because someone had come to take him away from that hellish place. I was a helicopter pilot, and that was my job. Nothing else mattered.

My heart ceased feeling as though it was going to crash through my ribs. My thinking calmed. I stopped worrying about rounds striking the aircraft. I concentrated on what I had to do.

"We're up," the crew chief called.

The takeoff took every ounce of power that the overloaded Huey could muster as it struggled to become airborne. I flew around the edge of a large clearing, hugging the tree line, and staying low to the ground until we had built our speed to about one hundred knots. Then I pulled the nose of the helicopter up, and we soared high into the air like a triumphant eagle that had snatched its next meal from the claws of a hungry bear.

I have no idea about the fate of that boy soldier, but I have always prayed that he made it out alive. His simple act gave me so much. I hope that I gave him something in return.

32
Twist of Fate

There is no armor against fate.

~James Shirley

May 27, 1968—Phuoc Vinh (*fook vin*), South Vietnam

"Bercaw, wake up."

Groggy I rolled over to see what was going on. Lieutenant Robinson was standing by my bunk, and it was still dark—never a good sign.

"What?"

"We've got a unit about five clicks east of here in contact, and they need an emergency ammo resupply."

"Shit."

Night missions always sucked—nothing good ever happen at night in Vietnam.

Sitting up on the edge of my cot, I said, "Okay. I'm awake. Make certain the crew has the aircraft ready."

"They're already on it," he replied.

"Morgan," I said to Jim, who was still asleep in his bunk. "Get up. We got a mission."

Grumbling Jim sat up on the edge of his bunk. "What now?"

"Don't worry. It'll be fun."

The sun was still below the horizon as I nursed the over-loaded Huey into the air. "Good thing it's still cool. We'd never get this pig off the ground later today."

Jim called to check for any active artillery, and I called the unit in contact.

"Alpha Six. Alpha Six, this is Eagle One-One-Eight. We have just departed Phuoc Vinh and are awaiting instructions."

"Eagle One-One-Eight, this is Alpha Six. Charlie has broken off contact."

"Thank the gods for that. We owe them one," Jim said.

"Roger, Alpha Six. I understand Charlie has broken off contact," I said.

"This is Alpha Six. Affirmative, and let us know when you want smoke, and land to the north staying as close to the south end of the LZ as possible. That is all we have secured."

"Roger that," I said. "And go ahead and pop that smoke."

After a moment, "Alpha Six, we identify red smoke," Jim radioed, pointing toward the little red cloud slowly rising above the trees.

"This might end up being a quick in-and-out mission," I said. "We just might make it back in time to get something to eat before our next mission."

Dropping below the tree line I worked to keep the airspeed around thirty-five knots so that we would not stall. I only started further reducing the airspeed as we neared the ground. Someone had chopped down several trees, most likely just minutes before, to give us an area where we could land. A soldier with his rifle raised over his head stood where he wanted us to touch down. All was lush, green, and rather peaceful-looking in the early morning light.

As the Huey approached an altitude of about ten feet, an unseen swath of small steel balls flashed across the LZ, slicing through everything in their path.[17] A wall of fire and black smoke raced immediately behind rolling from right to left and enveloping everything in sight. Reacting with an involuntary contraction of all of my muscles, I jerked the controls causing the helicopter to jump as if it had hit a bump. Everyone onboard thought we had been hit. Maybe we had been. The enormity of the explosion was shocking.

"Coming right! Clear me right!"

"You're clear. Bring it around." Jim sounded as if he were speaking through clinched teeth. The gunner rattled off the same information.

Trees were rapidly approaching, and the Huey, overloaded with ammo, did not want to climb. I pulled in all available power and the RPM started to bleed off. The helicopter, which was very close to stalling, began to shake.

"Airspeed is about twenty-two knots. Torque is forty-five pounds and climbing. RPM is about sixty-four hundred and holding," Jim said.

We hit the trees. The nose of the Huey smacked them loudly and then we dragged the skids through the tops. The aircraft jerked as it repeatedly snagged limbs that threatened to pull the helicopter down. Eventually we staggered into clean air and both the crew chief and the gunner reported that we had a couple of limbs hanging from the skids. The

---

17 Information eventually reached us that the initial explosion had been the result of Claymore Mines. I never found out if they were Chinese or some of ours captured by the enemy.

radios went wild, and I finally felt like I could pay attention to what was going on back on the ground.

"We have dead and wounded soldiers in the LZ." This was Alpha Six. "We need immediate emergency medevac."

"Roger. Let me get set up and we'll be back in."

Jim instructed the crew to place all of the ammunition in the doorways, and he told them to kick it out as soon as we cleared the tree line.

"Alpha Six, keep your people clear of our approach," I called. "We're going to dump the ammo as we come in. Over."

"Roger, One-One-Eight. We need you here as soon as possible."

"We're coming as fast as we can."

I had gone two or three miles south to give the crew time to get the ammo boxes positioned. Heading back, I established a long, shallow approach.

"Alpha Six, we're about a mile on final approach. Are you ready for us?" I radioed.

"Eagle One-One-Eight, this is Dustoff Four-Six. Over."

"Dustoff?" Jim said. "Where'd they come from?"

"This is One-One-Eight. Go ahead."

"This is Dustoff Four-Six. We're about one mile to your west. Why don't you let us go in and retrieve the most seriously wounded, and then you can go in, unload your ammo, and pick up the less seriously wounded and the dead."

"Dustoff Four-Six, this is Eagle One-One-Eight. That sounds good. Alpha Six, did you copy?"

"Alpha Six. Roger. Copy."

The Dustoff Huey came in from the direction of Phuoc Vinh, and the pilot made a left turn for a short final approach to the LZ.

Orbiting about two miles to the south, we waited for Dustoff Four-Six to call that they had cleared the LZ.

"I just saw an explosion down there," Jim said.

I turned the helicopter back toward the north to try to see what was going on in the LZ.

"Eagle One-One-Eight, this is Alpha Six."

"This is One-One-Eight. Go."

"Dustoff Four-Six has been destroyed by heavy weapons firing from the north. The LZ is now unusable." After a long pause with the radio still keyed, he said, "You might as well head back to base."

"Alpha Six, do you want us to drop the ammunition off somewhere?" My throat muscles were so tight that I was having difficulty speaking.

"No. We're okay for the moment."

"Roger. We're headed back. Good luck."

It was silent onboard the aircraft. I could feel my heartbeat in my stomach. All the adrenalin pumping through my body was taking a toll. It caused a sickness in my stomach that spread through my body. I pressed both feet hard against the pedals to try to hide the fact that my legs were shaking.

Finally, I said, "That should have been us."

"I know," Jim said.

After a moment, Jim said, "They stopped the attack because they knew helicopters would come out. That was a fucking ambush."

Jim called the tower for landing, and I called operations and notified them of our situation. After landing, Lieutenant Robinson told us that we had time to grab a bite to eat before our scheduled mission.

"Robbie, I hate to say this, but I really don't want to fly anymore today," I said.

After a pause, the lieutenant said, "Okay, I'll put another crew on it."

Jim and I opened the bar early that day.

Names on The Wall

Major William Joseph Ballinger
First Lieutenant Guy Bernard Ephland Jr.
Sergeant Kenneth Ray Rucker
Specialist 4 Alan Louis Matte
Captain Anthony George Prior

Rest in Peace[18]

18 Toward the end of 2009, Joseph Michael, a former infantry medic, put me in touch with Michael Ballinger, son of Major William J. Ballinger, the pilot of Dustoff 46. Michael, an Army medic, gave me additional information regarding this incident. As I understand it, an RPG struck Ballinger's helicopter (dispatched from Quan Loi) while attempting to hoist Captain Prior from the jungle below.

33
Dak Pek

There are no mistakes, no coincidences. All events are blessings given to us to learn from.

~Elizabeth Kubler-Ross

End of May, 1968—Dak To (*doc toe*), South Vietnam

"So, why are we doing this stupid shit?" Jim asked as we commenced placing one-hundred-mile-per-hour tape over the 101st patches on our uniforms and on the helicopters.

"We're trying to confuse the enemy," I said.

"Confuse the enemy? You mean so they'll fail to realize that we belong to the American military. And is it possible that the hootch-maid network has broken down, and they failed to pass along the info that we were moving north, or is there some other dumb-fucking reason I'm missing?"

"I think the answer is C—some other dumb-fucking reason."

"Someone told me that we're going north because the NVA are moving into the area with tanks—tanks, for Chrissake."

"Yeah, and all the gunnies are all excited about the rumor that they're coming in with helicopters. They all want to be the first to down a helicopter in air-to-air combat."

"Sure, that would be cool, and as soon as I see one, I'll be yelling at them to come save my ass," Jim said.

Jim and I received orders to move our helicopter forward to Dak Pek (*doc peck*) from Dak To. Neither of us was thrilled to be the only helicopter moving to a forward base of operations, especially with tank and helicopter rumors.

Dak To tower reported a two-thousand-foot overcast as we planned our route north. I checked the map and said, "As soon as we take off we should see a small stream. We turn right and follow it to a valley and eventually to Dak Pek."

"That seems simple enough," Jim said. It did seem simple enough for two experienced combat pilots.

Because of the movement of the 3rd Brigade and others into Dak To, airplanes and helicopters landed, departed, taxied, and parked all over the airfield. After a lengthy wait, I finally managed to contact the tower. I volunteered to stay low and get the hell out of the way as quickly as possible, an offer that the air traffic controller accepted. Immediately after takeoff, we spotted the stream, turned left, and began following it. Spotting the valley, we turned and flew into it happy to be clear of the airfield and all the traffic. So far, so good—or so we thought.

As we flew along, the valley became progressively narrower with a thick jungle canopy below. The cloud cover dropped rapidly until we found ourselves trapped between it and the walls of the valley. I no longer had sufficient room to turn the aircraft around while remaining clear of the cloud cover.

"You know, Mr. Bercaw, if anyone is down there with a big fat stick, they can just smack us with it," said the door gunner.

"Okay, your job is to keep your eyes open for men with large sticks."

With the thick jungle just a few feet below the helicopter, I was certain that in the event of an emergency landing no one would ever find us.

"I forgot my paddle," Jim said.

"Paddle?"

"Yeah, so we could get back down shit creek."

Fortunately, the cloud cover began to lift a bit, and to my great relief, we soon broke out of our claustrophobic canyon. We found ourselves in a vast panoramic valley framed with mountains in the distance and filled with rice paddies to the left and to the right. The low cloud cover gave the scene a violet hue, with the exception of a single break in the overcast about twenty miles in front of us. A brilliant shaft of sunlight beamed down from right to left, illuminating a fair-sized town. The heavens had opened and were pointing the way for us.

"I didn't realize that Dak Pek was so large. Did you?" I asked.

"Turn around!" Jim said, shouting into his microphone.

"What?"

"Turn around!"

I brought the helicopter around in a hard left turn, only to find several valleys facing me. I did not know which one we had just exited.

"What's the problem?"

"That's not Dak Pek."

"What?" At times, I am a bit slow on the uptake.

"We're in Laos."

"What?" Okay, sometimes I am very slow on the uptake. "Laos. Laos? How the hell did we get into Laos? Where's Dak Pek?"

"Just get us back to Vietnam before we start an international incident."

I picked a valley I thought might be the one that we had just flown through and headed back. Now we were lost, not that we would ever admit it. Tuning the frequency back to the Dak To tower, I watched the FM Homing device needle for the general direction back. It indicated that we needed to fly perpendicular to our present direction of flight, but given the mountains and the cloud cover, this was not possible.

"How *exactly* did you get us so far off course? Weren't you watching the map?" I said.

"Correct me if I'm wrong, but aren't you the aircraft commander, and didn't you tell me you knew where you were going?"

I did not remember saying anything like that.

And so it went, back and forth, giving our crew no end of confidence in our abilities as pilots. Later we determined that we had crossed the northern tip of Cambodia, west of Dak To before flying into Laos.

After an eternity, we reached the end of the valley and turned toward Dak To. Once refueled, we again headed out to Dak Pek. The second attempt proved to be successful.

Dak Pek, a small village that was far from the relative safety of the larger military bases, sat on the west side of the valley. It was in a green bowl of wild, mountainous, jungle-covered terrain. It was like an Asian version of a little town in the Wild West. The inhabitant's isolation must have been nearly complete until we Americans dropped in with all of our noise and our junk.

A small airstrip bordered the village to the east. Someone had built the runway by digging through a small hill, the remains of which stood guard on both sides of the northern end of the strip. From time to time, it snagged an airplane out of the air just after takeoff or just before landing. We witnessed an Air Force C-7A[19] that clipped the hill just before touchdown, ripping the left wing from the plane. The wing caught fire and the aircraft spun around as it slid down the runway. Fortunately, no one was seriously injured. About a week later, an article and photo appeared in *The Pacific Stars and Stripes* newspaper, explaining how the valiant Air Force pilots had skillfully landed the plane after sustaining damage by enemy fire. Early one morning, another Air Force plane clipped the hill and crashed during takeoff. Jim and I medevaced the seriously injured pilot.

A small group of Montagnard men and their families lived in a compound beside the runway. They were our first line of defense.

Ours was to be the only helicopter remaining overnight.

When we were not flying, we parked the helicopter on a pad built for us at the north end of the runway beside the Montagnard camp. Surrounded by sandbags and topped with concertina wire, their compound was strictly off limits to all U.S. military personnel. Considering the number of fierce-looking Montagnard men in the compound, this was not a problem for me. I enjoyed having all of my body parts intact.

Each evening when we were through flying for the day, I would sit out by the helicopter just a few feet from the

---

19 A smaller twin-engine cargo plane that the Air Force stole from the Army – but I digress.

concertina wire, eat some C-Rations, drink some coffee, and smoke. After one or two evenings, an attractive young Montagnard woman came up to the wire directly opposite me. Standing there, she began combing her long black hair while she watched me. I smoked and watched her until it became too dark for us to see each other. The next evening, she again stood tantalizingly close just across the wire, watching me and combing her hair. This became a surreal ritual that I found myself looking forward to each evening with growing anticipation. We did this every evening until I departed about two weeks later. I never dared to try to gain entry into the camp for my disemboweled body would have certainly been found outside the compound the next morning.

34
Night Mission

It's not enough that we do our best; sometimes we have to do what's required.

~Sir Winston Churchill

Approximately 0200 hours, June 1, 1968—Dak Pek, South Vietnam

"Mr. Bercaw. Mr. Bercaw, can you hear me?" the duty officer said, shaking me awake.

I had been sleeping on my air mattress, which had gone flat, in the back of the helicopter just behind the pilot's seats. The crew chief, Samsel, and the gunner, Ragland, slept on the ground by the aircraft. Morgan dozed somewhere inside by the operations center.

"Does anyone ever sleep the whole fucking night in this fucking country?"

"I'm sorry, Mr. Bercaw, but we have a seriously wounded man up in the mountains who needs to be medevaced immediately,"

"How bad is he?" I asked. "Can't this wait until it's light?"

"I'm told he's very serious."

Sitting up, I began to feel a bit guilty for complaining about lack of sleep when some poor grunt was lying out in the jungle wounded—perhaps dying. "Okay, give me a minute."

I stuck my head outside the Huey and noted a low overcast. "Middle-of-the-fucking-night mountain medevac with obscuring clouds. Good. I wouldn't want this to be too easy."

Neither the crew chief nor the gunner, who were already preparing the aircraft for departure, said a word.

"Do either of you know where Morgan is sleeping?"

"No," they both responded.

"One of you run back into the compound and see if you can locate him."

Already coughing as I lit a cigarette, I dressed in all of my flight gear and combat gear, and I buckled myself into the left seat. Soon Ragland ran back with word that he could not locate Jim.

"Okay. I'll start the engine. He'll hear that and come out."

I pulled the starter switch, the igniters started snapping, and the turbine began its slow whine as it reluctantly began to turn. It did not like working at night either. The swishing sound as each rotor blade passed by my door quickly turned into the unmistakable sound of a Huey at full throttle. Since ours was the only helicopter there I was certain that Morgan would come running. I waited for about five minutes and lit my second cigarette, wondering if they were causing my nearly constant headaches. Morgan never appeared.

"Did you look everywhere for Morgan?" I asked Ragland.

"I looked. I asked. No one knew where he was."

Well, shit. Already strapped into the left seat and not feeling like changing over to the right side, I decided to fly the mission single pilot from the left seat.[20] There were already so many things wrong with the mission that only a fool would take it. With unwarranted faith, the crew chief and gunner climbed onboard and buckled in.

The overcast engulfed me almost the instant I left the ground. Leaning a bit to the right so that I could use the full set of instruments on the opposite side of the Huey, I climbed through the overcast and into a clear night sky filled with an astonishing number of stars.

All I had was a radio frequency and a call sign.

"Charlie Six Alpha. Charlie Six Alpha, this is Army Helicopter One-One-Five. Over."

"One-One-Five, this is Charlie Six Alpha. We're here. Over."

"Roger. I'm coming to pick up your medevac, but I need your location. Over."

"One-One-Five, we are about five clicks due south of the runway at Dak Pek. Over."

I kept circling over the airfield while climbing to about one thousand feet above the valley floor.

"Charlie Six Alpha, can you pop a flare for me?"

"Roger. Stand by."

After about a minute, I spotted the flare arcing out about one thousand feet up on the west side of a mountain that was approximately three miles to the south.

Normally at night, I flew with no lights except for the rotating beacon to avoid becoming a target, but now I reached over and switched on the landing light, the searchlight, and

20 Due to the configuration of the instruments, the pilot is supposed to occupy the right seat when flying the Huey single pilot.

the running lights. We probably looked like a Christmas tree. I hoped that the troops on the ground would be able to clearly see us and avoid the main rotor and the tail rotor.

"Charlie Six Alpha, can you call artillery and have them put a big flare or two over the area?"

They did. The million-candle-power flare burst into existence like a miniature sun ensuring that every enemy soldier within ten miles knew that something was up.

"Thanks. Have them keep 'em coming until we tell them to stop."

During the approach, I scanned the area, hoping to find somewhere to land that was far enough out from the side of the mountain that I would not strike it with the rotor blades. No such luck. I was going to have to try to hover over one thousand feet up the side of a mountain while they loaded the wounded soldier onboard.

I had three choices. I could fly around the mountain to the left in the dark and come in for an into-the-wind approach. I could swing out to the right, risking hitting one of the flares and turn back into the wind. Or I could make a downwind approach. The super-bright light from the flare had destroyed my night vision, so I could see nothing except for the illuminated area. The flare, which was drifting lazily down under an oscillating parachute, created pirouetting black shadows. Eventually, the flare drifted down into the valley placing the light source below the landing zone, creating a phantasmagorical scene that intensified my headache. *Maybe the call for flares had been a bad idea*. Gripping the controls so tightly that my fingers hurt, I decided not to fly around in this mess just to line myself up for a textbook approach. I opted for the downwind approach. I*n for a penny, in for a pound.*

Ponchos and the soldiers who had rigged them for shelter clung to a small space on the side of the mountain.

"Charlie Six Alpha, have your troops try and secure their gear unless they want it blown away." I knew it was a futile effort, as I was entirely too close and they would not have the time.

To the crew chief and the gunner I said, "Let me know if I get too close to anything. Watch the blades on the left side—and of course watch the tail rotor. Keep an eye on the troops so that they don't run into the blades, and let me know if I start drifting away from the spot."

Immediately my extemporaneous plan began to unravel. Ponchos and equipment swirled into the air, and a couple of soldiers fell to the ground, knocked down by the terrific winds that the rotor blades created. Terrified that someone might fall off the mountain or that the equipment flying around might damage the rotor system, I came to a very high hover.

Once at a hover the helicopter tried to weathervane itself into the wind. Every time a wind gust hit us, the tail of the Huey blew up into the air. I had to pull in full aft cyclic to keep from drifting away from the spot. I tried not to think about the main rotor flexing down and severing the tail boom—disastrous for everyone. I did my best to smooth my movements of the controls as I descended as closely as I could to the mountain. The Huey began to rock from side to side, as men began clambering up on the left skid to prepare to load the casualty. In addition, I had another problem. With nothing in front of me to use as a reference for maintaining a stationary hover, I was forced to look at the mountain to my left, where wild shadows and whirling blade tips danced among the rocks and trees. Boulders that were visible some distance below beckoned me down to join them. I suppressed a momentary image of the Huey cartwheeling down the mountain and spewing men out into the night. I took some comfort from the thought that death would almost certainly be quick.

After what seemed like an eternity, Samsel called, "We're up."

"Clear on the right?" I asked Ragland.

"Sir, there ain't nothin' on the right 'cept a thousand feet of nothin'."

"I'll take that as yes."

As I began to depart, the last parachute flare burned out, and our small world plunged into nearly total blackness. I made a rapid and shaky transition to flying via the instruments. Burned-out parachute flares still floated toward earth somewhere in front of me, and I began a hard right turn to stay clear of them.

"Keep me clear to the right," I instructed Ragland. "I can't see a damned thing in that direction."

Flying visually to ensure that I did not run into a mountain and using the instruments so that I would not put the aircraft into a dangerous flight configuration, I continued the turn and began to climb another thousand feet, hoping that the extra altitude would give us a little more safety. I relaxed a bit as the valley and the overcast, now below us and brightly reflecting the moon's light, came into view. It was time to face the next problem on my checklist. How was I going to land?

Fortunately, I had the tower frequency for Dak To memorized. I climbed another thousand feet to ensure that we would have reliable radio communications.

"Dak To Tower, this is Eagle One-One-Five. Over."

"Eagle One-One-Five, this is Dak To. Go ahead."

"Roger. What are your weather conditions?"

"We are zero-zero with no departures or landings."

"Okay, thanks."

Crap.

I also remembered the frequency for the Camp Holloway tower. It was close enough that I could reach it with the fuel I had onboard.

"Camp Holloway Tower, this is Eagle One-One-Five. Over."

"Eagle One-One-Five, this is Holloway. Go ahead."

"What are your weather conditions?"

"We are zero-zero with no departures or landings."

Shit! I took a deep breath.

"Okay. Could you check Pleiku (*play koo*) or anyplace else close to see if I might be able to get in?"

After a couple of minutes, he said, "Eagle One-One-Five, Pleiku advises that their weather's the same as ours."

Struggling to remain calm, I analyzed my situation. A low overcast hid the landing pad at Dak Pek, and the same overcast blanketed all of the surrounding airfields within reach. I did not have enough fuel to stay in the air until morning, and even if I did, I still might not be able to land. I considered finding a spot in the mountains that was big enough to land the helicopter. From there, we could wait until we could go elsewhere. My only other choice was to go to an airfield with a GCA and let them talk me all the way to the ground. Hopefully, I would see the ground before I actually made contact with it.

I called the radio operator on the ground at Dak Pek so that I could verbalize my situation with someone outside of the aircraft.

After listening to me he said, "Sir, we have a big searchlight outside of Operations. Would you like me to turn it on for you?"

I thought about this for a moment. "Can you tell me how low the overcast is at your location?"

"It is up around a thousand feet or so," he said.

Since we had been at about one-thousand feet above the ground just a few minutes ago, I knew that this was not an accurate estimate.

"Can you take a look outside and tell me if the clouds are touching anything like trees or poles or antennas?"

After a long pause, he said, "No. It's not touching anything."

"Okay then. Is it possible for you to drag the searchlight down beside the helicopter pad, point it straight up, and turn it on?"

"Roger. We should be able to do that. I'll be off the air for a few minutes."

After an interminable period, he said, "Eagle One-One-Five, it's on."

I looked down, and there it was, a faint bluish circle painted on the clouds below me. I took a full breath—probably my first since this mission had begun. So far, so good. Now for the scary part. "Got it! Verify the exact position of the searchlight, please."

"It's sitting right beside the pad on the west side."

"Thanks. Can you have some people standing by to receive my medevac and to be available to help just in case this doesn't work?"

"Roger that. We have quite a few people waiting on you."

My simple plan was to descend down to the top of the overcast, slowing my airspeed down to around thirty or forty knots as I descended, keeping the beam of light off the left side of the Huey. I reasoned this would keep me near the landing pad. Since the radio operator had told me that the overcast was not touching anything like the tops of trees or towers, I was hoping to have a moment when we would see the ground before hitting anything.

"Okay. Listen up," I said to my crew. "Let me know the second you see anything, and tell me specifically what you see and where it is in relation to us. Okay?"

I began the descent. The entire operation worked far better than I had any right to expect, and we broke out in the clear approximately one hundred feet above the ground. I did not even have to make a turn before landing. Although I was about fifty yards beyond the helicopter pad, I shut down the engine where we landed. I did not intend to move it anywhere for the rest of the night. My muscles ached, and my fingers hurt as I loosened them from the controls.

"Mr. Bercaw, look at this," Ragland said.

Turning in my seat, I watched our patient walk away from the helicopter. How serious was he? I was too exhausted and too happy to be safely on the ground to be very upset over the fact that I had just risked all of our lives in the middle of the night for someone who did not appear to be injured. I was not even upset that this was the second dangerous medevac mission I had flown to extract someone who appeared to be neither ill nor wounded.

The next morning, while I sat on my deflated air mattress in a foul mood, smoking my first cigarette and still nursing a headache, Morgan came strolling out to the aircraft. He was whistling. That was too much. I went nose to nose with him, "Where the fuck were you last night? Didn't you hear us start the engine?"

"I was sleeping up by the TOC. I woke up once when I heard a helicopter landing and asked myself, 'What kind of asshole is out flying at night in weather like this?'"[21]

---

21 I received the Distinguished Flying Cross for that night mission—presumably, for not destroying the aircraft and killing everyone onboard during a questionable operation.

35
C-Rations

"Take thine ease, eat, drink, and be merry."

~**Luke 12:19 (King James Version)**

June, 1968—Dak Pek, South Vietnam

Sitting in the dirt by the helicopter, I tore open the case of C-Rations that we kept for ourselves from a load we carried earlier in the day. In a flurry of hands, I managed to grab the first box that caught my eye. It was a box of "Beans w/ Frankfurter Chunks in Tomato Sauce." This was not what I wanted, but it was highly desired, and I could trade it for a different meal. I preferred the "Ham and Eggs, Chopped," and I had no trouble convincing a crew chief to trade with me. Few others appreciated this meal, possibly due to its gray color with a hint of green. I seldom had any difficulty obtaining it.

More often than not, I ate my meals cold—sometimes while flying. That evening, however, we were finished flying for the day, and we could invest the time to make the meal more enjoyable. Sitting in the powdery dirt with my crew, I opened the box and removed all of the contents: the can containing the ham and eggs, a can of sliced peaches, and a can called the B-1 Unit. It contained crackers, chocolate candy, a small tin of peanut butter, and a foil accessory packet that contained four cigarettes, moisture-resistant matches, chewing gum (two Chiclets), a personal-size roll of toilet paper, instant coffee, non-dairy creamer, sugar, salt, and a plastic spoon.

With my P-38, I opened the B-1 Unit. The P-38, an ingenious little device that consisted of a rectangular piece of stamped metal grooved down the center for extra strength, was just big enough to grasp firmly between the thumb and the forefinger. A small hole allowed almost every soldier in Vietnam to attach one to his dog tag chain, even if he never used it. A notch in the side placed over the rim of the can gave leverage. A claw-like blade swung out ninety degrees to the handle, and by rotating the device back and forth, the can opened with relative ease.

After opening the B-1 Unit and removing the contents, I cut a series of air holes around the can just below the rim. Then I filled it about two-thirds full with dirt. I handed the can to Morgan, who had already crawled under the helicopter to fill his dirt-filled can with JP-4 fuel from the drain valve. I now had a very effective stove with which to heat my meal. The dirt, having absorbed all of the fuel, made it unlikely that an overturned can would splash burning fuel all over the place.

Opening the can of "Ham and Eggs, Chopped," I took care to leave a small section of the lid attached. Folding it into thirds provided me with a handle. With the supplied spoon, I loosened the contents a bit and added some water from my canteen.

As the water began to a boil, I mixed it with the eggs and ham until they were beyond chopped—mashed would be a better term. I bartered for some cheese, which was included with some of the other meals. I mixed the cheese in for some added flavor. Some of the infantry guys obtained items like Tabasco Sauce from home giving their meals extra flavoring. C-Ration meals provided a minimum of 1,200 calories, and they were rather good, especially after the variety of menus increased sometime in early 1968. Unfortunately, the number of menus was still limited, and I became bored after I had gone through everything a few times. Additional problems, especially if your job required you to hump gear through the jungle, were that C-Rations were heavy, noisy, and they took up a lot of space.

After finishing the entrée, I ate the peaches—always a treat. I ended my meal with instant coffee, which I added to heated water in my canteen cup. I sat back and opened the cigarette pack of Salem Cigarettes—more often than not, it was Salem. Tearing the filter off to reduce the menthol taste, I lit the cigarette and leaned back against the helicopter's front skid cross tube. I ate the candy, which was not too bad. However, the quality of the chocolate frequently suffered, as it was often dry and cracked. At the end, while chewing the gum, we raided the remainder of the case, taking what we wanted and throwing the rest away. We would liberate another case from the many that we would undoubtedly haul sometime the next day.

36
Arc Light

Such sheets of fire, such bursts of torrid thunder.

~William Shakespeare

June, 1968—Early morning, northwest of Dak Pek, South Vietnam

Flying over a series of ridgelines and narrow valleys that reminded me of a Japanese folding fan, Morgan and I followed ten Hueys strung out before us in a loose trail formation. They were descending in a long, sweeping arc on the final approach of a combat assault. Jim was doing the flying. Colonel Mowery and members of his staff monitored the assault from our aircraft. The ships were widely spaced, as the LZ was only big enough to land one helicopter at a time. Situated under a low cloud cover, the dark LZ sparkled with little twinkling lights, the result of gunships firing high-explosive shells into the area. The whole scene was rather picturesque. War can be fiercely beautiful.

As the first of the Hueys prepared to land, one of the gunships radioed that they had spotted personnel on the last ridgeline prior to the LZ. A crewmember on the gunship had thrown a red smoke grenade to mark the spot. As our helicopter flew over the area, we observed several men looking up at us. While continuing toward the LZ, watching the final helicopter discharge its human cargo, Colonel Mowery called the commander on the ground and notified him that we were going back to take a look at the men on the ridgeline before returning to land.

Jim made a right turn and called the gunships to notify them of our intentions. As we turned to the east, each ridgeline rose as a dark shadow above the blue haze that rested in the narrow valleys. The grandeur of Vietnam moved me once again. Having had the privilege of seeing Vietnam from the Delta in the south to the mountains in the north, from the endless unspoiled beaches along the coast to the exhilarating, vibrant streets of Saigon, I found it to be a beautiful and exciting country.

Continuing our right turn, we spotted the last wisps of the red smoke grenade, and everyone was keen to identify the men on the ridgeline. I instructed the gunner and the crew chief to be alert and to have their guns at the ready. Intently peering ahead for any indication of danger I peripherally picked up a couple of flashes of light off to my left. I turned my head to observe what appeared to be a series of explosions some distance down the ridgeline.

"Jim, what the hell is that?" I asked, pointing toward the explosions and thereby triggering a moment of absolute insanity.

Jim threw the helicopter into a violent diving right turn. The maneuver vaguely resembled a Split-S—something that fighter aircraft perform. Diving into the valley he began a recovery that had the Huey shuddering from the strains placed on it. Startled by the violence of the maneuver and still trying to understand what was going on, I managed to say something useful like, "What the fuck?"

The colonel and his staff added their own obscene exclamations from the rear of the helicopter. One or two of the staff moved forward to do something (I can only imagine what they had in mind). Trying to get myself back in control of the situation, I attempted to reach the microphone switch to ask Jim just what he was doing. Since he was usually an ultra-safe pilot, he had shaken me with his actions.

As he continued the steep turn back to the direction from which we had started everyone onboard the aircraft, me included, grew very quiet. Before us, the earth had opened and the fires of hell spewed forth. Flames boiled up from the ridgeline, mixed with smoke that was so thick and black that it appeared to be solid, like a chunk of molten metal as it begins to cool.

"What the *fuck* is that?" I yelled.

"It's a fucking B-52 strike!" Jim said; his tone indicated that I was a complete idiot for not knowing.

"A B-52 strike? A B-52 strike! Did we know about this? Were you briefed on this?"

"No. Didn't you receive the briefing?"

I had. There had been no mention of a pending Arc Light mission in our area.

Jim got the aircraft under control again just as Colonel Mowery spoke. "Take us back to the pad." He was referring to the helicopter landing area back at Dak Pek.

The colonel had a major assigned as the S-3 (Air) to coordinate all aviation activities in the brigade's area of operations including B-52 strikes. Awaiting our arrival, this unfortunate major stood beside the landing pad in the position of attention that was as rigid as any private standing before a drill sergeant. Colonel Mowery looked every bit like a colonel, and when he exited the aircraft, he must have resembled the angel of death descending upon the hapless major. I was very happy not to be in his shoes.

Looking back on the situation, I realize that we were only seconds from death. Had it not been for the valley that Jim nose-dived into, the concussions from the explosions and possible shrapnel would have likely damaged or destroyed our Huey. Had the strike not hit exactly on the top of the ridgeline, thus depriving us of the safety of the valley, I would not be writing this. Neither the colonel nor any member of his staff ever said a word to us about the incident. The fates and identities of the men we had spotted on the ridgeline were sealed in one horrific moment—a moment of fierce beauty.

37
This Just In

It does not require a majority to prevail, but rather an irate, tireless minority keen to set brush fires in people's minds.

~Attributed to Samuel Adams

June 6, 1968—radio broadcast out of Saigon, South Vietnam

"Robert F. Kennedy died early this morning…"

"What the fuck?"

"…from wounds received when he was shot early yesterday morning after giving a victory speech in Los Angeles, California."

"What the fuck is going on back there?"

"We will keep you updated as more information arrives."

"Seriously, what is going on back there? Riots, murders, assassinations, protests, draft-dodging chickenshits … fuck it! I mean, just fuck it!"

38
Control

Perfection is finally attained, not when there is no longer anything to add, but when there is no longer anything to take away.

~ANTOINE DE SAINT-EXUPERY

Mid-June, 1968—South of Phuoc Vinh, South Vietnam

"Let's see you make this approach with minimal control movements."

"Is this a challenge?" I asked.

"Yeah," Jim said. "I want to see you set the collective and not have to touch it until landing."

"Okeydokey, trainee," I said. "Watch and learn."

We were around twelve hundred feet above the ground and about a mile west of the smoke the troops had popped for us. A large open area lay between our position and theirs. It was still early morning, relatively cool, and the smoke rose straight up into the air indicating little or no wind. Currently headed south I projected an imaginary line from our position that followed the tree line around the southern border of the clear area in a gradual descent terminating at the dwindling smoke. Now all I had to do was follow that line.

Reducing power as smoothly as I could and pulling the cyclic back slightly and to the left, I began the approach. The key to backing up my arrogant comment was to make only minimal movements with the cyclic until completing a smooth landing—hopefully.

A light haze in the quiet air gave an easy peaceful feeling to the morning, which I found hard to believe was not real. Not for the first time, the thought ran through my mind that I could do this kind of flying for the rest of my life if it were not for the high-risk-of-getting-killed part of the job.

I still visualized that imaginary line, and the helicopter slid right down it like a rollercoaster riding the track. It took us around the southern edge of the clearing, and since we made a good target with this kind of purposeful performance, I hoped no bad guys waited in the tree line for a cocky pilot to wander by.

Engine noise, transmission whine, and popping rotor blades all blended into a comforting background sound. The Huey responded to my thoughts. My control touch, which was exponentially better than it had been on my first mission so long ago, could sense the tiniest of the aircraft's movements. We were one. Sex should be as good.

We continued to follow the line, and I still had not moved the controls.

Jim looked back at the crew chief. "Don't worry. He'll screw it up at the bottom."

"Oh, ye of little faith," I said.

Down around three hundred feet I thought that the air-speed might be a touch high, but I was determined not to move the controls until I had to. I hoped that this would spare me the scorn of the crew—especially Jim. I edged the cyclic back an amount that was so small that I hoped no one would notice. I spotted the soldier standing with his rifle held over his head, indicating the spot where he wanted us to land, and my imaginary line terminated exactly at that spot. *Good. Really good.*

The hard part, the landing, was coming up. I approached more quickly than the Army had taught in flight school because I did not want to fall below translational lift until the last possible moment. I would have welcomed a good headwind. Down we came, and I felt the first tiny tremors of translational lift. I eased in an infinitesimal amount of power and moved the cyclic forward an equal amount to carry the approach forward to the desired spot. We were nearing that spot very quickly, and I had to get it all exactly right, or I would spoil this beautiful approach and for the remainder of the day I would have to listen to Jim telling anyone who would listen about how I screwed it up.

Holding off until what seemed like the last possible moment, I added a little more power, lowered the nose just a bit, touched down like a whisper, and slid about two feet. The Huey rocked forward slightly as we came to a complete stop.

Beautiful.

"Not bad," Jim said.

"Hopefully, you learned something by observing my superior piloting skills."

I received no comment, but few things in life have given me as much pleasure as that approach and landing. I would never again duplicate it with such perfection.

39
The Body

And another of his disciples said unto him, "Lord, suffer me first to go and bury my father." But Jesus said unto him, "Follow me; and let the dead bury their dead."

~Matthew 8:21-22 (King James Version)

Mid-June, 1968—Vicinity of Cu Chi (*coo chee*), South Vietnam

"Eagle One-One-Six, this is Bravo Six Alpha. Over."

"This is One-One-Six. Go."

"Roger. Bravo Six wants to know if you can take a few things we have picked up back to HQ. Over."

"One-One-Six, roger."

"What do you suppose they have?" the copilot asked.

"Beats me, but we'll find out."

We landed in an area of knee-high grass and a few scattered trees. Several soldiers approached from our right side carrying all sorts of military items. Two men farther back were carrying what looked like a body. One of the soldiers walked around to my side. I swung my microphone boom out and keyed the intercom switch so that I could hear him talking.

"The lieutenant wants you to take that stuff back to HQ to be analyzed. There's also a dink body. Take it back with the other stuff."

"Jesus, sir. This body stinks to high heaven," the door gunner said.

"It'll only be a couple of minutes, and we can get rid of it."

Landing at the headquarters site, I called and asked for troops to unload the equipment and the body.

"Body? What body is that?" the radio operator in headquarters asked.

"The body that your unit asked us to bring back to you along with all of the other gear that they loaded on us," I said.

After a pause, he said, "We don't want the body. Take it to the morgue."

After landing at the morgue, a couple of troopers ran out to see what we wanted.

"Hey, that's a gook body," one of them said. "We don't take no gook bodies."

"I was told to bring it here."

"Sorry, sir, but we only take American bodies."

I placed a call back to headquarters, "The morgue won't take the body. What am I supposed to do with it? Over."

After a pause, "I don't care what you do with it, but we do not want it."

"Well, what the fuck! What the hell are we supposed to do with it?" the copilot asked.

"I don't know," I said. "Anyone got any ideas?"

"Let's just dump it somewhere," the crew chief said.

"Dump it? Where?"

"Somewhere over the fence."

"We can't do that," I said.

"You have any other suggestions?" the copilot asked.

"Well, shit. This sucks."

"If you got a better idea, fine, but that's all I got."

I brought the helicopter down to a hover just outside the perimeter fence. It wobbled a bit as the gunner moved around and pushed the body off into the high grass.

"We're clear," he said.

"Wonderful. Just fucking wonderful," I said. "I hope someone takes better care of me when I go."

"Nah," the copilot said. "We plan on dumping your ass right alongside Charlie back there."

40
This Ain't No Shit

To be a person is to have a story to tell.

~ISAK DINESEN

Early June, 1968—ARVN compound south of Phuoc Vinh, South Vietnam

The cockpit lit up as if lightning had struck. A puff of black smoke followed, rising from a hole in the ground just below the chin bubble on my side.

"What the hell was that?" my copilot Hagan asked.

"I don't know," I said. "Some sort of explosion."

I had already started to take off for the safety of altitude. We had been sitting next to one of the many small ARVN compounds found throughout South Vietnam. Shaped like an equilateral triangle, they were supposed to be easy to defend, but in reality they were too small, too isolated, and undermanned by poorly disciplined troops. In fact, many of the troops may have been NVA sympathizers, and they may have fired on us from inside the compound.

"You okay?" Hagan asked.

"Yeah. Check the instruments."

A moment later, he said, "Everything seems to be okay."

"Jesus! I don't think we received any damage. Whatever that was—an RPG?—either hit inside a hole or it went underground before it exploded. Jesus. What luck."

I told our passenger, a major, that we were returning to Phuoc Vinh to see if we had sustained any damage. Once back on the ground, the major decided he did not want to fly anymore and he left. While looking for damage and finding none, Lieutenant Robinson and Jim Morgan approached and told me that I had an emergency resupply mission right back in the area I had just departed from. For reasons I have forgotten, Morgan replaced Hagan as my copilot.

Our destination was a unit deployed along a tree line just north of the ARVN compound. We were briefed that the area was possibly hot—another bit of information for my no-shit folder.

We identified the LZ early on, and since it was not far away, I decided to stay low and come in hot and fast. I did this as much for show as for any combat consideration.

Skimming along just above the ground and roaring in straight toward the line of trees was exciting, especially for the folks onboard who possibly did not appreciate my masterly piloting skills. At the last moment, I hauled the nose back to make a very rapid deceleration. The nose was high enough that I had to look straight out through the chin bubble to see where we were landing. I noticed that we had picked up a passenger. An unfortunate snake, about five feet long, caught up in the powerful downwash from the rotor system, tumbled end over end like a gray stick right in front of us. I hate snakes.

"As soon as we hit the ground, you guys start throwing that stuff off," Jim ordered the crew.

Because I was fixated on the snake, we landed rather hard, and the snake flailed around about ten feet out in front of us. The damn thing actually came completely off the ground at times. I guessed it was pissed, and I was glad I was not out there with it.

As I watched the snake and waited for an indication from the crew chief that we were ready to depart, a Vietnamese man wearing civilian clothes and carrying a burlap bag ran toward us from our left front. Running up to the left side of the helicopter, he threw the bag into the open cargo door and kept on running out of sight.

"Throw that off," Jim yelled.

"What the hell is that? Is he one of ours?" I could not see what was going on behind me.

"Throw it off. Throw the goddamned thing off," Jim yelled to the crew chief.

"It's off. It's off!" the crew chief yelled back.

"Get out of here. Now!" Jim yelled at me.

"What do you think was in the bag?" I asked.

"I don't know, and I don't care."

Lifting the helicopter up, I had to back up a bit to get out from under the trees. The renewed downwash got the snake all riled up again. When I got high enough to clear the trees, I made a left pedal turn and headed back to Phuoc Vinh. Besides scaring the major and pissing off the snake, I do not think we accomplished much that day other than racking up another war story.

41
Running Departure

I cannot believe that the purpose of life is to be happy. I think the purpose of life is to be useful, to be responsible, to be compassionate. It is, above all to matter, to count, to stand for something, to have made some difference that you lived at all.

~LEO ROSTEN

Early June, 1968—somewhere between Phuoc Vinh and Cu Chi, South Vietnam

"Eagle One-One-Eight, can you make a quick pick up for us?"

"This is One-One-Eight. What do you need? Over."

"One-One-Eight, we have a squad of men with gear who need a ride. They are north of Cu Chi. We don't want to leave them out there overnight."

"Ah, roger. Give me the location."

With another Vietnamese day fading away, we proceeded in the direction of the grid coordinates to retrieve the stranded squad. Fortunately, the map indicated that they were located in a large open area that should be reasonably easy to find in the fading light.

"What the hell is a squad of men doing out here with no plan in place to bring them home?" asked the crew chief.

"It's probably just another army fuckup," said the door gunner.

A half hour later, we dropped down into a rather large LZ, and I thought I could see approximately twelve men with gear on the eastern side near the tree line.

"Jesus," the copilot said. "How are we going to get this many troops on this thing?"

"I don't know. I'm guessing that no one wants to spend the night out here, so we can always have them ditch their gear if necessary."

Turning on a short final approach, I said, "Keep your eyes open, guys. Let's make certain these are really Americans."

We landed on the east side of a large clearing facing in a northwesterly direction. Men immediately started clambering onboard. I could hear equipment banging against the helicopter and men grunting and cursing. I realized too late that I should have instructed them to clear their weapons.

"Try to get the men as far back as possible. Put the packs up front for weight and balance," I said.

After a bit more noise, "Sir, we've got one guy left. We can't get him on," said my door gunner.

"Okay. Why don't you tell him that he has to stay here tonight."

"Sir?"

"Look, I don't care what you do. Let him sit on your lap, just get him onboard."

After a noisy pause, "Okay, we're up," said the gunner.

"You think this thing will fly?" asked my copilot.

"I dunno. Let's try it."

The top two or three feet of the trees were still in sunlight as I began to increase the power. The Huey did not move.

"What are my readings?"

"We're at 103 percent power."

"Really?"

"Yes."

I pushed against the left pedal. Nothing happened. I pushed a little harder, and then even harder. Finally, the aircraft gave a jerk and then turned about ten degrees to the left. Then I pressed the right pedal until we had turned about twenty degrees back to the right. Pressing the left pedal again, I centered the nose of the Huey between the two extremes.

"Woo. Shit. Okay. Here we go. Watch the instruments."

Thinking back to my first flight in Vietnam and the running departure with Captain Hudson, I eased the cyclic forward a bit. After a moment, we began to slide. It was bumpy and the aircraft began rocking from side to side. The grunts began to hoot and holler as if they were on a carnival ride. Apparently, they thought I had everything under control.

"What happens if we can't get airborne," asked the copilot.

"Then we'll have them throw some of their gear off."

After what seemed to be a very long time, we broke ground, flying along just inches above the dirt. After a few seconds in the air, we struck a small rise in the ground. This slowed the helicopter enough that we descended and hit the ground again with a thump and then another thump. Once again, we staggered back into the air.

"What do the instruments say?"

"You don't want to know," said the copilot.

I managed to keep it in the air this time. We gained altitude and airspeed very slowly, and I had to turn and head south, continuing to run along the tree line.

"What's our plan?" asked my copilot.

"We're going to keep circling this LZ until we get enough altitude to clear the trees. Why? Do you have a better idea?"

Slowly we clawed our way above the trees just before I had to turn again.

"Sir, the blades are coned up pretty good," said the crew chief.

"Okay, keep me posted … are we in any danger?"

"No. I think we're okay."

As we continued our slow climb into a rapidly darkening sky, we eventually saw the lights of the big base at Cu Chi beckoning with the offers of food, rest, and safety.

42
A Pink Mist

Nothing in life is so exhilarating as to be shot at without result.

~Sir Winston Churchill

Approximately 1215 hours, June 18, 1968—North of Cu Chi, South Vietnam

The last yellow puffs from the smoke grenade drifting up from the small jungle clearing indicated that there was a slight wind coming from the south. Surrounded by about fifty feet of relatively low jungle growth and taller trees, the open area was just barely large enough for one Huey. A couple of GIs stood in the open, one of them waiting to guide us in for the landing.

"Let me take this in," Jim said. "I need some practice with high overhead approaches."

"You have the controls."

This was a routine mission. Troops on the ground had captured a bunch of the enemy's equipment and had asked us to pick it up so that they would not have to carry it.

Jim turned until we headed generally south, the direction he intended to land. Once over the clearing, he reduced the power to begin a rapid descent, executed a right-hand turn and began reducing the airspeed. Moments later, we were on short final approach for landing.

The soldier on the ground held his M-16 in both hands horizontally over his head to indicate where he wanted us to land. As we got closer, he lowered his weapon letting us know that we were where he wanted us to be and that we were clear of all obstacles. Once we were on the ground, our crew chief Dave Wendt and our gunner Guy Jacobsen both jumped out to assist with the loading of the equipment. I turned in my seat looking over my right shoulder, and I watched them throw in everything from weapons to bicycles and some other junk that I could not identify.

The angry chatter of an automatic weapon startled me as it started firing somewhere to our rear. Turning to look out my door, I saw one soldier standing about twenty feet from us. Seemingly alarmed, he was looking rapidly from left to right. Wendt and Jacobsen both jumped back on the aircraft. Turning back to the right I stretched my right leg toward the intercom's floor switch. I was planning to tell Jim to climb to the relative safety of altitude until we determined exactly what was happening.

Wham.

Wham. Wham. Wham.

Bullets slammed into the front of the aircraft. It seemed like the instrument panel exploded. Shrapnel ricocheted around hitting me in the face. For a moment, I thought I actually saw the bullets.

Jesus, Jesus, Jesus. I tried to make myself small.

Wham.

My right leg flew into the air. My body, following my leg, twisted violently to the right. I yelled so hard that it felt as though something solid had ripped through my throat. All of this seemed to be happening to someone else; I was just watching. Fully aware that I might be witnessing the end of my life, I braced for additional impacts.

As Jim began to take off, one of the enemy soldiers stood up in front of us, opened fire, and ventilated the bottom of the Huey as we flew over him.

When we were barely two hundred feet in the air, the engine began surging rhythmically and making rather frightening noises. We started losing altitude. Looking to my right I saw Jim making huge, erratic movements with the controls. As a result, this made unsustainable demands on the rotor system, and the helicopter began settling into the jungle. *Jesus Christ.* I was supposed to be in charge, and I needed to do something. I placed my feet on the pedals and my hands on the controls.

"Jim. I have the controls."

The words had an immediate calming effect on him. The noises ceased and we began to climb back to altitude.

"No," he said. "I'm okay now."

"Okay. You have the controls."

I began to worry about myself again. Blood, astonishingly red, ran down from under my pant leg and over the heel of my boot. At that point, I knew at least one bullet had hit my knee, and my leg hurt so badly I felt certain I was seriously injured and possibly crippled. Unable to remember any pressure points, I put my hands around my leg just above the knee and squeezed to try to stop the flow of blood.

Reaching forward with my foot, I keyed the intercom's floor switch, "Jim, I'm hit."

That is the first time, I believe, that Wendt and Jacobsen realized I was wounded.

"I know. I'm going to get you to the hospital as soon as possible. And congratulations. You got yourself a Purple Heart."

I felt unreasonably pleased with this statement, but for the moment, I wondered if my flying career was over.

"I'm bleeding like a son-of-a-bitch," I said.

"Jake," Jim called to the gunner, "come up and take a look at Mr. Bercaw."

Jim said something to Jake over the intercom about an artery and cutting the leg open so he could close it off. Then Jake leaned over me with the biggest knife I had ever seen. The whole thing scared the shit out of me.

"The bleeding has tapered off," I blurted out. It had slackened, and I did not want Jake anywhere near me with that knife.

"Jake," Jim said. "Pull him out of the seat and take a look at his wounds."

Jake opened the two release levers behind my armored seat, tilted the seat back, and he dragged me out onto the floor of the cargo area. Feeling rather foolish, as I had now decided that I was not going to die, I scooted myself clear of the seat using my elbows and my good leg.

As Jake pulled me out, I looked back where Wendt was sitting, ashen-faced. Later, after inspecting the aircraft, we discovered that two bullets had struck the aircraft by his head. One of them was about one inch from the right side of his head and the other one was about one inch from the left side of his head. Fate favored him that day.

Once I was on the floor Jake again brought out that knife, and once again, it scared the shit out of me. Now disconnected from the intercom I could not hear any of the conversation between Jim and the crew. However, after some gestures between us, which probably involved a look of stark terror on my part, Jake helped me understand that he was just going to cut my pant leg off. *Great.* These were brand new jungle fatigues. They actually fit me and this was the first day I had worn them. Still struggling with the concept that someone had tried to kill me, I failed to realize that the pant leg he intended to cut off was soaked in blood with a bullet hole through it.

Jake finished cutting the pant leg off. Then, after conferring with Jim, he retrieved the first-aid kit installed just behind my seat. These kits were made of a heavy canvas material with a heavy-duty zipper. The zipper stuck, so Jake grabbed the kit with both hands and ripped it open. There was an overabundance of adrenalin onboard that aircraft.

He placed two compress bandages so that they covered the outside of my leg.

"No," I yelled at Jake, pointing to the entry wound, a small puckered opening on the inside of my leg.

He shook his head and pointed to the other side. I leaned to my right. The exit wound was a large ragged hole that provided a view into the interior of my leg. There was also another wound further up on my thigh. Apparently, the bullet had entered near the front of my leg, exited behind my knee, traveled along the side of my leg for a bit, then, as we eventually determined, continued through the aircraft, and struck Jake's machine gun. I began to feel very lightheaded, and I decided to lie back and let him work.

My stomach knotted as the bottom dropped out, and we entered a rapid descent. *Now what*?

"What the hell is going on?" I yelled at Wendt.

"We're on fire," he yelled back.

Jim took us down to treetop level so that he could get us on the ground as quickly as possible when it finally became necessary. However, we were over heavy jungle, and I doubted that there were many prime landing areas available. Now pissed off because I had allowed Jake to take me out of my seat and disconnect me from the communications system, I nonetheless lay back down deciding that Jim was doing the best that he could under the circumstances. Jake continued to work on my wounds.

Jim called Cu Chi tower and notified them of our situation, requesting that they have medics and emergency equipment standing by when we landed. Then, for reasons I have never fully understood, he decided to land at our usual confined-area helipad, instead of out in the open, where the emergency equipment would have had easy access to us. I have asked him about this decision several times over the years, but he gets testy and I have decided to forgive him for it.

Once we landed, we all exited the helicopter quickly. It turned out that we were not on fire. However, because we had been shot several times as we flew over the enemy soldier, fuel, hydraulic fluid, and other liquids had leaked out of the belly of the aircraft. Once these liquids hit the air at around 115 miles per hour, they vaporized, and to Wendt this appeared to be smoke. The final drops of fuel drained out through the bullet holes within minutes after landing. Jim assured me later that he had been monitoring the fuel loss, and he had determined that we could make it safely back to Cu Chi.

A fire truck, the only piece of the emergency equipment that managed to find us, transported me. Jim managed to get me into a hospital without female nurses. I have never forgiven him for that.

Orderlies carried me into the emergency room on a green canvas military stretcher and placed it on two sawhorses. By now, my knee and upper leg had become numb from nerve damage,[22] but my lower leg and my foot hurt like hell. I could feel every beat of my heart acutely in my foot, which slowly turned blue and then purple. My mind reeled trying to piece together all that had just happened. It took nearly three days before I managed to sort out the sequence of events that afternoon. I am still not certain that I have an accurate recollection of the events of that day.

Lying on the stretcher, I felt like I should have some sort of special attention. In addition, I had left my cigarettes in the aircraft and I needed one badly. I asked a corpsman for one. He gave me a nearly full pack. As I lay there smoking and considering my newly acquired status as a genuine wounded war vet, I looked over to my right. On a stretcher next to me was a young Vietnamese girl who appeared to be about twelve years old. She had a large hole blown through her right thigh. Lying there and watching me, she appeared quite calm. I smiled, but she just kept watching me. I began to feel rather foolish.

Eventually, orderlies took me to a room that was completely bare except for a metal table in the center. They placed me on the table on my belly. A corpsman came in, I had yet to see a doctor, and offered me some milk and cookies. I had not had milk and cookies since I was a child. He then explained that he was going to numb my leg, and he

22 The nerve damage would continue to plague me for more than twenty years.

did so with a series of shots. He and an assistant then started doing things to my leg involving rubbery cutting sounds that I really did not want to hear.

At one point, he asked if I would like to see what they were doing. I looked back over my shoulder at the exit wound behind my knee. The hole was much bigger than it had been the last time I saw it and a lot of white stuff, muscle tissue I believe, surrounded the area. For the second time that day, I felt very lightheaded. I turned my head back around and tried to concentrate on the cookies. The corpsman walked around in front of me holding what looked exactly like a cleaning rod for a rifle.

"I'm going to run this through the wound to clean it, and you might feel some discomfort when this happens," he said.

"Okay."

I believe I groaned. It hurt, a very deep to-the-bone hurt.

"Sorry," he said. "For now, I'm just going to bandage you. We won't sew you up for a few days, until we are certain that there is no infection."

"Okay."

Wheeled to my ward, I found that in addition to not having female nurses it did not have a working air conditioner. By now, my foot throbbed to the point that I could not ignore it, and I simply could not stop thinking about the events of the last couple of hours. I kept going through each step in minute detail. My mind was demanding to know exactly what had happened.

It pleased me to note that access to the bunker was next to my bed. That was good. Sweaty and naked, a young soldier fitfully sleeping in the bed beside me had balls the size of baseballs. I never asked what caused that condition, but I hoped it was nothing contagious. It seemed that everyone in my ward had relatively minor wounds or ailments. I assumed that the lack of air-conditioning had precluded the placement of any seriously wounded people in our wing.

Shortly thereafter, a group of people, including Morgan, came to visit me. Everyone inquired as to what had happened. In pain, exhausted, still confused, and not really in a visiting mood, I was not certain what to tell them.

Jim, agitated and obviously still experiencing an adrenalin rush, said, "John, you should have seen it. I just happened to be looking at you when you were hit, and a pink mist just exploded from your leg!"

For the third time that day, I suffered a bout of lightheadedness.

On the afternoon of my second day in the hospital, a young soldier two bunks to my left asked, "Are you someone important?"

"What?"

"Who are you? You get so many visitors."

"Oh. No. No, I'm just a pilot, but we find it easier to get around than most people. Anyone who stops here at Cu Chi makes the trip to say hello. That's all." I started to feel guilty, as most of my ward companions were enlisted infantrymen who never received any visitors.

One of the patients kept asking the medics for his status. He desperately wanted to get out of the hospital so that he could return to his unit. He felt a huge responsibility to the other men in his outfit, and it bugged the hell out of him that he was not there to do his part. I thought he should just lie back and enjoy the break he had bought and paid for. Like most helicopter pilots, my sense of responsibility was not so much to my unit but to the men on the ground.

Three days later, I finally had my only visit from a doctor. He looked at my wound and decided to sew me up. As the medic wheeled me off to another room, I wondered how they were going to sew up the very large hole in the back of my leg. Were they just going to sew the skin down around the edges of the wound?

They answered this question quickly by pulling both sides of the wound together and then stitching them. The shortened muscles no longer allowed me to straighten my leg. I required a month of painful stretching exercises before I could fully straighten it and return to flying.

43
Time Off

Passion, it lies in all of us.

~Joss Whedon

Late July, 1968—Phuoc Vinh, South Vietnam

Searching in vain for any shade, I pulled my cap low over my eyes for some protection from the sun, which always seemed to be directly overhead. I struggled to take a full breath as warm, humid air filled my lungs. My jungle fatigues, clinging to my body as if they had just been washed but not dried, hampered every step. Little whirlwinds danced around, swirling dust up into my eyes, nose, and mouth, which was so dry I could not work up a good spit.

Armed with a bottle of rum, Milo Overstreet, Al Fritz, and I headed for a bar located just outside of the military gate. Constructed of some thick, heavy material and painted white to help protect it from the sun, the bar sat about twenty-five feet away from the road. Built from the same material, a low, white fence sat at the edge of the street guarding hard-packed earth where nothing grew. Young women, ranging in age from too-young teens to the early twenties, beckoned us to join them as we approached. The building provided immediate relief from the glare, but not the heat. Instead of cooling us, a big fan only angered the humidity.

Selecting a table as far from the door as possible, we ordered Cokes and glasses with ice from the bar girl who approached us as soon as we sat down.

"No, no," she said, waving her hands back and forth at us. "You no bring own booze."

"Don't worry about it, sweetheart," Milo said. "We're buying the Cokes."

"No, no," she continued, as she hurried off to find the manager.

The manager, a tiny, hard-eyed woman of indeterminate age, seemed to be satisfied with our assurances that we would spend plenty of money before the day was over.

Milo opened the bottle and generously poured rum into each glass.

"Cheers," he said, extending his glass over the table.

"Cheers," Al and I said, as we all clinked our glasses.

Feeling the warm glow in my belly that resulted from pouring booze into an empty stomach, I poured another round as the muscles in my neck and shoulders began to relax. By the third drink, I began to feel the mellow, all-is-well feeling, along with the looseness of thought and the fuzzy vision that comes from consuming too much alcohol in too little time.

Small rectangular windows set high in the walls filtered the light. Along with the rum, this gave the room a false sense of peacefulness and security.

"How the hell did all three of us manage to get a day off together?" Milo asked.

Al shrugged. "Beats me."

"A lifetime of clean living," I said, eliciting a chuckle from the others.

We began a rambling period of conversation about all of the things that young men talk about as we watched the women and drank the rum.

An attractive young woman who was probably still in her teens sat down at the table across from me so that I was able to look at her without turning my head. She had dark, though not black, hair cut short with a curl framing each of her ears. She wore black silk pants and a white blouse with the top button open so that I could see just the beginning of the swell of her breasts.

Drinking something that looked like iced tea, she made the slightest glance in my general direction. Though she never looked directly at me, she knew that I was watching her, and like good-looking women everywhere, she was aware of her effect on men. Displaying the faintest self-satisfied smile, she sat brushing her right forefinger lightly across her lips. Completely captivated, I stared unashamedly.

"Did you guys hear the rumor that we're going to be sent back north?" Al asked.

"Yeah, I heard Morgan talking about it," I said and turned my attention back to the girl.

Milo glanced over his shoulder to see what had my attention. Turning back, he smiled approvingly. "Watch out, Johnny. She's probably a VC, and she'll cut your balls off."

"Well, I haven't been using them much lately, anyway." We all laughed.

I returned to watching the girl, and Milo and Al's conversation faded into the background. A delicate sheen of perspiration painted her skin with an erotic glow. My fingertips tingled as I tried to imagine how it would feel to touch her. A small bead of moisture slipped from her hairline behind her left ear and began a tantalizing journey down her neck like an early-morning dewdrop wending its way down a flower petal. Traveling in a tiny zigzag path, the droplet stopped, gained enough additional moisture to overcome inertia, and trickled down until it again halted and then repeated the process. Months had passed since I had been this close to an attractive woman and the battle between friction and gravity for control of that little rivulet of moisture became the center my universe.

The glistening droplet paused upon reaching the shallow area above her collarbone until it created a tiny pool that spilled over only to stop again when it reached the hollow at her throat. Once more, it pooled and then trickled over, continuing its little twisting path down between the rising mounds of her breasts and eventually disappearing behind her white blouse. Dizzy from alcohol and desire, I found that the heat and humidity that had so dogged me before, now held me in a sensual embrace. The warm air filling my lungs became something that I relished.

With every sense heightened, each breath I took echoed within my head, and I wondered if anyone else could hear it. Ice tinkling in glasses across the room had the soothing and rather sensual quality of a woman's laughter heard from a distance on a warm summer evening. The light playing upon her skin produced subtle shades of color that seemed almost psychedelic. My fingertips found a rich sensuality in the moisture coating my drink glass. It became the sheen on her skin, tantalizingly just out of reach. The faint scent of a musky perfume wafted across the table, and my thoughts sank deeper into a sensual frenzy. A sip of rum and Coke exploded in my mouth, sending little bubbles skittering along the sides of my tongue and down my throat. I needed to touch her—I needed her to touch me. Power and pressure surged through my body demanding release.

Now deep in alcohol-fueled sexual euphoria, I thought I could almost taste her breath. My body felt hot. Surely, if she added her body heat to mine, we would spontaneously combust.

Unfortunately, this did not happen.

Another woman, approximately the same age, came and sat with her for a moment. After a short animated conversation, the two of them prepared to leave. The girl stood, turned her head, and looking directly at me, gave the slightest of smiles before walking out into the sun and heat, leaving me in a mental state of coitus interruptus. My ardor turned into frustration, irritation, and anger over things that I could not control. Pissed off, I returned to the primary business of the day: drinking.

44
Flaming Hookers

In life, each of us must sometimes play the fool.

~YIDDISH PROVERB

Late July, 1968—Officers' Club, Phuoc Vinh, South Vietnam

Milo, Al, and I finished the rum and consumed more than our share of the Vietnamese 33 (*Ba M' Ba*) beer before roaring all over town spreading American goodwill. As curfew approached, we headed back to camp where Jim Morgan joined us, and we moved to the officers' club after determining that we needed more alcohol.

"Let's play liar's dice for drinks," Jim said, as we took seats at the bar.

"How do you play that?" I asked.

"Bartender, let me have the dice cup," Jim said. "Honestly, what have you boys done with your lives? I mean, who doesn't know how to play liar's dice?"

He dumped five dice contained in the leather dice cup onto the bar.

"First, all players throw one die. The highest gets to go first."

Jim placed the dice back in the cup. "Then the winner shakes the cup and upends it on the bar like this."

He slammed the cup down on the bar. Based on his demonstration, it seems this works best when the cup contacts the bar surface at the same moment the player utters a profane exclamation of his choice. Jim then looked at his dice by using the cup and his free hand to shield them from our view.

"This game is played like draw poker. For example…" He removed the cup to expose a three, two fours, a five, and a six. "I have a pair of fours with a six high."

"Ah, poker with dice," Milo said. Milo was—and still is—an avid poker player, prompting Al to nickname him Hi-Lo Milo.

"Then what?" Al asked.

"Well, just remember that this is called liar's dice. You can tell the next player the truth, or you can lie and make up a hand that is either higher *or lower* than what you actually have."

"And then?" I asked.

With infinite patience, Jim continued with his instructions. "The next player can accept what he has been told and try to beat it, or if he is unable to beat it, he can try to bluff the next player."

"That's it?" Milo asked, sounding a bit disappointed.

"No. Another option is to challenge the previous player."

Milo cocked his head. "Challenge?"

"Yes. If challenged and the player has a hand lower than the one he announced, he has to take a drink. But, if challenged and he does have what he stated – or, of course, better – the challenger has to take a drink."

"Ah," Milo said, interested once again. "A drinking game involving dice *and* poker."

We all agreed that this sounded good, and we started playing. However, we quickly tired of the game and made some modifications.

"This is boring," said Al, his speech beginning to slur.

"What do you suggest?" said Jim.

"Just count the aces you have. The seventh ace, say, will name a drink. The eleventh will pay for it, and the twenty-first will drink it."

"Good. That's good," I said.

"Can't the same person end up doing all three things?" Milo asked.

"That will just make it more interesting," Jim replied.

Later, we changed the rules again so that the fifteenth ace consumed the drink. Apparently, we could not get alcohol into our bodies quickly enough.

Later, the inventive Mr. Morgan came up with another modification to the game. "Let's do Flaming Hookers."

"Flaming Hookers?" I said.

Turning toward the bartender, Jim said, "Bartender, bring me a shot of Rémy Martin Cognac."

Once it arrived, Jim continued his instructions. "The object is to light this on fire, drink it down, place the shot glass back on the bar, and *if you are really good*, there will still be a wisp of flame at the bottom of the glass."

"That's really, really good," I said.

Milo agreed.

Frowning, Al said, "Let's see you do it."

Jim lit the fire, downed the shot, and then with an exuberant "Ha!" he slammed the shot glass down on the bar. Exuberance enhances any experience.

"You have to do it as soon as the fire is started," he said. "Otherwise, the liquid will become too hot. Also, be careful not to set your mustache on fire." Safety is always an important consideration for any new venture.

This little antic quickly drew a crowd, and other officers, both pilots and non-pilots, joined us. One time Jim became a bit high-spirited, and we witnessed liquid fire running from both corners of his mouth, down his neck, and disappearing into his shirt. This drew rousing cheers from everyone, along with calls for another demonstration.

As the evening wore on, and it became Morgan's turn to name a drink, he decided he was bored with Flaming Hookers. It was time to liven things up.

"Bartender, please make a drink of George Dickel Whiskey."

This proved to be a popular choice, as we all thought the name Dickel was hysterical.

But he wasn't done. "Also, include a shot of Crème DeMenthe … and a shot of sausage water."

The bartender looked confused. "Sausage water?"

"Yeah," said Jim, excited by his choices.

Standing on the footrest of his bar stool, he leaned over the bar and pointed to the large jar of pickled sausages standing on the shelf on the back wall. "That stuff," he said.

Much later in the evening, it degenerated to triple shots of sausage water. That was probably a good idea, as it involved no alcohol.

Boredom has a way of creeping up on revelers. Late in the evening or early in the morning, one of the paratroopers climbed up on the bar and leaped, or possibly fell, off shouting "Geronimo" before he hit the floor. What a wonderful idea. Almost immediately, we all stood on the bar waiting for our turn to demonstrate our individual skill at the time-honored tradition of bar jumping. The bartender kept yelling something about the bar not supporting all the weight, but we cheerfully ignored him.

Leaping from the top of the bar, the paratroopers had a plan at least. When they reached the floor, they executed a drunken parachute-landing fall. The pilots, not to be outdone, conducted autorotations. We just jumped from the bar to the floor hoping that tomorrow would not involve the discovery of broken body parts—kind of like a real autorotation.

Later, while it was still dark, I found myself outside in a squatting position. Unable to stand, I experienced a moment of panic when I realized that I could not feel my legs, and I was lost. Forcing my pickled brain to concentrate, I slowly located myself, very generally, based on sounds and a familiar-looking building. However, no signals passed between my brain and anything below my waist preventing me from standing. Eventually, I must have leaned to one side, as I fell over and lay there for quite a while until the shooting pains in my legs subsided, and I thought I might once again be able to use them for their intended purpose.

The faint glow of a new day showed on the eastern horizon as I made it back to my bunk and scratched one more day off my short-timer calendar.

45
On the Job Training

Human beings, who are almost unique in having the ability to learn from the experience of others, are also remarkable for their apparent disinclination to do so.

~Douglas Adams

Late July, 1968—North of Cu Chi, South Vietnam

The day had already run on too long, and now with darkness nearly upon us and with storms approaching, we received a call asking if we would do one more mission. A small unit, located about twenty miles north, requested we move some captured enemy equipment back to the unit headquarters at Cu Chi. Morgan and I received the same type of call on the day that I was wounded. Both units were located in the same general area, and I was flying the same aircraft—bad karma, indeed.

I agreed to accept the mission, even though little superstitious alarms were going off in my head, and I wanted to return to Phuoc Vinh for the night before the storms moved into the area. Having just returned to flight status, I still struggled to get my confidence back to pre-wound levels. Additionally, I had worked all day with an aircrew that was new to Vietnam. The copilot's attitude was that he knew all about flying because he had spent some time flying in the states before coming to Vietnam, and he felt that he did not need instruction from someone who had not been flying for much longer than he had been.

Assigned to support a unit at Cu Chi for the day, we had conducted many ash-and-trash missions. The copilot's response to most of my observations on flying in Vietnam was, "We didn't do it like that back in the States."

Having picked up a host of bad habits in a very short period, he no longer even adhered to the basic helicopter control that the Army taught us in flight school, apparently believing that these techniques were for beginners only. The crew chief and the gunner brought their own set of bad habits and attitudes to the day. Mainly, they sat back in the corner of their cubbyholes and slept. By the time we received the request for one last mission, I had developed an attitude of my own.

Heading north, while we flew around little ribbon-like rain showers glowing in the setting sunlight, we kept an eye on the storms that were moving in from the west. The always-ominous jungle looked even more foreboding as darkness crept across the land. As we neared the ground, I glanced back at the crew. As expected, both the gunner and the crew chief were leaning back with their eyes closed.

"You guys want to get on your guns back there? We *are* landing in the jungle."

Like moody teenagers, they sat up and brought their guns to the ready positions.

"And if it's not too much trouble, how about some clearing information."

This brought some half-hearted responses from both of them.

"Just in case I haven't *yet* made myself clear on this point, there are *no* fucking passengers on this aircraft—everyone works."

Upon landing, soldiers threw various pieces of enemy equipment onboard. The gunner and crew chief remained seated, not showing any inclination to assist. I was too tired and disgusted to say anything. The last items that were loaded and placed on the floor directly behind the copilot's seat were what appeared to be a complete set of china dishes. A lone 25th Infantry Division sergeant also came along.

The sun dropped out of sight, and one large storm, which was just visible in the fading twilight, loomed between us and Cu Chi. I opted to run around the north side of it before heading back south. This kept us flying over somewhat safer and more familiar territory. At night, I usually ran with all of the lights off except for the rotating beacon. I hoped that this would make it harder for the enemy to target me, but it would still give other pilots the opportunity to see me before we collided. Unlike the United States, in Vietnam there were no city lights, highway lights, cars, or anything lighted to give visual cues as to your location, altitude, or aircraft attitude. It was like flying blindfolded. Along with the usual dangers, add a few other aircraft flying around with no lights, the possibility of a hidden storm or two, and it became very exciting. This type of situation was one of the many subjects on which I had briefed my copilot during the day.

Trying to get around the storm as quickly as possible, I flew closer to it than I would normally have, and this restricted our altitude to no more than six or seven hundred feet. The little alarms in my head got a bit louder.

My copilot leaned forward and started switching on all of the lights: the running lights, the searchlight, and the landing light. We were positively glowing in a heavy downpour.

"What the hell are you doing?" I asked.

"I want to make certain that other aircraft can see us."

"Turn those damned lights off! Don't worry about other aircraft; we're well below a thousand feet and fully in the dead man's zone.[23]

"It just seems safer if we can be seen," he said.

Boom. Boom. Boom. A large caliber weapon, most likely a .51 caliber, opened up accompanied by the chatter of AK-47s. They had seen us.

Wham, wham, wham. We started taking hits. The first round came up through the floor and through the map tucked between my seat and the radio console. Another round struck the dishes. The china seemed to explode sending fragments ricocheting around the inside of the aircraft. Slamming the collective down I nosed the helicopter over and dove for the tops of the trees. The infantry sergeant threw himself onto the floor with a thud and commenced firing his M-16 out into the night. With the rotor blades popping loudly, I made an abrupt recovery from the dive about ten feet above the jungle. This generated enough g-forces that it felt as though my face would pull away from my skull.

---

23 We generally flew below fifty feet or above 1,500 feet. Anything between these altitudes was dangerous, as it was well within range of most small-arms weapons, and this gave the enemy time to aim.

"Cu Chi Tower, this is Army Helicopter One-One-Eight, about twenty miles to your north. We've encountered heavy automatic weapons fire, and we're taking hits."

I wanted someone to know where we were in case we went down.

"Army One-One-Eight, roger. You are cleared for approach. Are you requesting emergency equipment?"

"One-One-Eight, stand by."

"Anyone hit?" I asked the crew.

Everyone responded in the negative.

"Gunner, why didn't you open fire?"

"Uh, I fired a couple of rounds and my gun jammed."

"I didn't hear you fire anything. How come your gun jammed? Couldn't you clear it? Is it clear now?"

I received a mumbled response.

"Chief, why didn't you fire?" I asked.

"My gun is jammed too."

"Bullshit!"

"Anyway, I couldn't see anything to shoot at."

"Just shoot. Maybe the sound will cause the other guy to duck. All we need is a couple of seconds to get clear. The two of you are fucked up, that's the problem. All three of you are fucked up. You think you know everything, but you don't know shit. You people are going to get yourselves killed—worse, you're going to get someone else killed. How is that, infantry guy?"

When I looked back, I could see the sergeant dimly in the last glow of light. I gave him a thumbs-up. He smiled and returned it.

"Cu Chi Tower, we took some hits, and I think we're losing fuel. I'm going to land at the north end of the runway and shut down. I'll have our people come out and take care of things."

"One-One-Eight, roger. You are cleared to land."

I popped up to enough altitude to put us on a normal approach. Making a quick call to our operations back at Phuoc Vinh, I gave them our status and requested someone to come pick us up. Once we were on the ground, I had the copilot shut the aircraft down while I called our Cu Chi operations to update them about our status.

"I thought we were hit and going down," the copilot said.

"So did I," the crew chief agreed.

"Me too," the gunner chimed in.

"Well, given the situation, we easily could have been. Did you hear that big gun? I'm really too short for this shit, and I certainly hope you guys learned something out of all of this."

46
Blood

There came a blinding flash, a deafening roar,
And dissonant cries of triumph and dismay;
Blood trickled down the river's reedy shore,
And with the dead he lay.

~ELBRIDGE JEFFERSON CUTLER

1968—Somewhere in South Vietnam

The Huey hit the ground hard, rocking forward, and then skidding for about two feet. Swarms of men immediately surged forward carrying wounded and possibly dying American soldiers. The crew chief and gunner jumped from the aircraft to assist with loading the men and their equipment. The sounds of battle echoed just beyond some trees a short distance to our left. After less than a minute, the crew chief climbed in and said, "We're up."

Looking out my door, I saw soldiers, bent forward at the waist, trying to keep themselves concealed in the tall grass as they ran back to the action.

Turning the controls over to the copilot, I turned so that I could see all of the wounded. Their bodies were torn and bleeding. Some faces reflected fear and pain; others reflected relief. Blood seeped, spurted, oozed, or bubbled from wound, mouth, nose, or ears. Dark and foreboding, it clung to anything and everything and glistened obscenely on soaked, dirty uniforms now stained almost black.

One trooper labored for each breath, his chest covered in froth. It looked like someone had splashed pink bubble bath on him. Bright-red blood pooled on the stomach of another soldier, but the edges had begun to turn almost black—visually insistent as it dried and darkened. I tried to breathe through my mouth, but the air, heavy and rank with blood's metallic scent, coated my tongue leaving a taste that I could neither shake nor forget.

We landed and again men swarmed us and began dragging the wounded from the aircraft. Where a man had been, blood remained, smeared and streaked across the battleship-gray floor as if some mad artist had created an expressionistic painting with wild, broad strokes using only shades of red.

The crew chief came to my window. "Mr. Bercaw, do we have time to wash the blood out?"

It was important to clean the aircraft as soon as possible. Otherwise, the blood seeped down between the floor plates into the belly of the helicopter among the cables, the wires, and the rods, where it rotted rapidly in the heat and humidity, emitting a stench that caused those exposed to struggle between the mutually exclusive actions of not breathing and retching. Life habitually requires that someone clean up the messes we leave behind. War is no different.

47
Bringing Home a Friend

Good men must die, but death cannot kill their names.

~PROVERB

August, 1968—Camp Eagle, South Vietnam

"Bercaw," Captain Kearns, the operations officer yelled at me. "Suit up and head out to the A Shau to bring Higbee's crew back."

The A Shau (*aw-shaw*) Valley, which was about twenty-five miles west of the old capitol city of Hue, South Vietnam, was the scene of some vicious fighting in 1968 that involved the 1st Cavalry Division and the 101st Airborne Division. Enemy forces, carrying supplies down from North Vietnam via the Ho Chi Minh Trail, traveled through the valley.

The bodies of Captain Gary Higbee and the crew of his gunship, killed while trying, all too successfully, to draw fire away from other troops, remained where they had fallen three days previously. American forces had a difficult time making it to the crash site.

In the 101st warrant officers felt that they were superior pilots and seldom trusted commissioned officer pilots. Commissioned officers considered warrants to be unruly children whom they had to tolerate due to the demand for pilots that the war had created. However, I respected Gary who was a hands-on pilot and not a desk jockey.

"We finally got men on-site to secure the area until we can retrieve the bodies," Kearns continued, "but they don't want to stay any longer than necessary, and they definitely want to be out of there before nightfall."

This would be my first mission in this area of operations since late March. I started to feel a bit apprehensive.

With a crew that I did not know and without taking the time to brief them on the procedures that I expected them to follow while in the aircraft, we headed west. Various fire-support bases lined the valley that led to the A Shau. My copilot pointed out several new bases built since I had last flown in this area. I noted their position, name (most were named after WW II battles involving the 101st), and radio frequency on my map for future reference. Crossing the ridgeline that marked the eastern boundary of the A Shau, we flew over an entire North Vietnam Army convoy that had suffered the extreme bad luck of having taken a direct hit from an Arc Light.

The last time I had flown into this area, it was all lush green jungle with a couple of trails and an abandoned airfield. Now its appearance shocked me. Countless bomb craters pockmarked the area, and long Arc Light slashes crisscrossed the valley floor. It was nearly unrecognizable. The abandoned A Luoi (*uh louie*) airfield had apparently been the center of intense fighting as the bomb craters overlapped each other, leaving almost none of the ground untouched. Large areas of the valley were devoid of vegetation. Dirt roads that had previously been undetected ran everywhere.

Crossing the ridgeline, I nosed the Huey over and plunged down the side of the valley leveling off at about fifty feet above the ground. My briefing had warned of anti-aircraft weapon positions situated throughout the valley and in the surrounding mountains. Therefore, in addition to other hazards, we all had to be alert for other helicopters that would be sharing the same small airspace while zooming around at 115 miles per hour—give or take.

Unidentified people flashed by beneath us as we zigged and zagged around the valley hoping to avoid enemy fire while moving in the general direction of the destroyed gunship.

My copilot gave me instructions to keep us on course. "Do you see that little hill at two o'clock?"

"Got it."

"Higbee crashed just on the other side."

Turning toward the hill, I pulled back on the cyclic control to slow our airspeed and gain altitude. However, when I reached the top of the hill I spotted troops below and I realized that I was too fast, too high, and too close. This would require me to make a nearly vertical approach. It seemed like a bad idea to make a go-around and come in for a second approach, as this would give the enemy the chance to down another helicopter in the same area. I bottomed the collective to reduce power and lose the remaining altitude, and I began a big flare to bleed off the rest of the airspeed.

"Your RPM is high," said the copilot.

I tried to control it. The landing was not pretty.

The bodies were loaded in a remarkably short time, and I commenced takeoff, intending to retrace our route out of the valley. Almost as soon as we were airborne, the stench hit me. It stuck in my throat and brought tears to my eyes. Desperate to take an untainted breath, I kicked hard on the right pedal causing the nose of the Huey to swing to the right. I was essentially flying sideways, allowing fresh air to flow through the aircraft.

"What the hell is that?" I yelled.

"It's the bodies, sir," the gunner said, his voice muffled.

Puzzled, I glanced back at the door gunner. He was covering his nose and mouth with his hand. Unfortunately, because of the way I flew the helicopter, the stench blew directly into him.

"Maybe fire support base Bertchesgarten has body bags they'll let us have," the copilot said.

A hurried radio call confirmed they had bags and would assist us. I quickly climbed out of the valley and landed in an open area in the center of the firebase, which was located on the top of the ridgeline. Troops converged on the aircraft as soon as we touched down. For the thousandth time, I was glad that I was a warrant officer, which spared me from an unpleasant task. Shamefully, I sat in the aircraft assuming my position as pilot-in-command and let lower-ranking men handle the task of placing the bodies into the body bags.

Turning in my seat, I was surprised at the condition of the bodies. They were bloated and waxen-skinned with uniforms stretched to the point that I feared they might burst at any moment. It took me a second to realize that this was the result of them having been in the jungle for three days. Gary—I could see him laughing at some stupid joke the last time I talked with him—had somehow become a body I could recognize only by the name on his uniform. When I think of him now, he is always laughing.

48
Turbulence, Centipedes, and Dragons

We think, sometimes, there's not a dragon left.

~Richard Bach

August, 1968—the mountains west of Camp Eagle, South Vietnam

The nose of the Huey was swinging violently ninety degrees left of center and then all the way back to ninety degrees right of center. The airspeed fluctuated between zero and over the red line. As far as my altitude was concerned, I just tried to keep us away from anything hard.

"Are you sure other Hueys are out in this stuff?" I asked.

"Yeah. We don't quit until the Chinooks quit," my copilot said.

"This is crazy," I replied.

"Yes, but we have to uphold the honor of Huey pilots everywhere."

"I hope they put that on my gravestone. 'His balls were bigger than those of the Chinook pilots,'" I said.

We were flying in the low mountains southwest of Camp Eagle. It was another gray and gloomy day. The turbulence was violent at best. Whether there was turbulence or not, our services were, as always, in constant demand.

"Where are we taking these C-Rations?" I asked.

"That's it—dead ahead," the copilot replied, pointing to a barren area on top of a low mountain that was probably inaccessible without the assistance of a helicopter.

I called for smoke to judge the prevailing wind. Someone tossed a yellow smoke canister onto the landing area. The copilot and I stared at it in utter amazement. It began swirling in a constant circle. We could see the canister actually spinning.

"I'm guessing there's no good way to approach this," I said, struggling to keep the Huey stable as we approached the small landing area.

"And there's no wrong way either."

Just short of touching down, some movement in front of me caught my eye.

"What the hell is that?" I asked, looking down through the chin bubble.

Scurrying rapidly ahead of us was something that looked like a centipede, except that it was huge. I estimated it to be about a foot and a half long. The body was dark gray and the legs were bright red. I banged first one skid on the ground and then the other trying to avoid hitting the thing. The centipede stopped for a moment, then took off, and quickly disappeared over the side of the mountain.

"Man. I'm glad I fly and don't have to live with stuff like that," I said.

With the C-Rations unloaded, we departed and headed for our next stop. This time we were going to pick up some personnel who were heading back to the U.S. of A. The firebase was located along the main route, which ran west toward the A Shau Valley. This site was even more inaccessible. Sitting on top of a small peak was a little crude building that I assumed to be living quarters and a couple of artillery pieces. There was no more room available. An even smaller landing area was exactly large enough for the skids of a Huey. A narrow, treacherous path that dropped off precipitously on each side separated the two areas. Undoubtedly, only the sure-footed or the foolhardy occupied this place.

"Who finds these places?" I asked.

"Most likely someone who never actually spends time in them."

"It looks like something out of some kid's fantasy story. I expect to see flying monkeys coming at us."

The turbulence on the approach intensified as we neared the tiny landing area. I tried to bring the Huey to a hover over the pad, but it was a lost cause. Finally, I slammed the helicopter down on the ground. We were facing about forty-five degrees left of the intended landing direction.

"Sir," the gunner yelled over the intercom. "This guy is signaling that he wants you to align the helicopter with the pad."

"Screw him. The next time this helicopter leaves the ground, we're departing."

The gunner made negative signs to the man on the other side of the path. Looking disgusted, he made his way along the path with his arms straight out to his sides while taking quick short steps, one foot in front of the other. Another soldier, using the same method to balance himself, quickly followed. Both of them were wearing bulky backpacks, carrying their rifles in one hand, and holding some sort of gear in the other.

"I bet that path is pretty scary," said the crew chief, as he leaned over and twisted around so he could see the action.

As soon as the two men were safely on board, we departed bouncing our way through the air heading back to base.

"Look at this! Look at this!" the gunner yelled.

I looked back at him. He was pointing to our right front.

I looked and saw a dragon.

It was sandy-colored and running flat out along a ridgeline that ran perpendicular to our direction of flight. I turned and followed it. The top of the ridgeline was barely wide enough for the creature, and the sides were so steep that only low vegetation grew on it, but the dragon never hesitated in its headlong flight. It looked exactly like my idea of a dragon,[24] or maybe a dinosaur, except that it was not green and it had four long legs and a long tail that stuck straight out in back as it ran.

"What *is* that?" someone exclaimed.

"Take a picture. Take a picture," I said. "Has anyone got a camera?"

No one did.

We followed along for a while. The dragon never slackened its pace.

The crew chief unfastened his seatbelt and moved around so he could see. "Anyone got any idea what this thing is?" he asked.

"It's fucking weird, that's what it is," said the gunner.

---

24 If I ignore the long legs, I think it might have been a komodo dragon.

49
Super Typhoon Wendy

Tropical Storm Wendy, which formed on August 28th in the open Western Pacific, quickly intensified to a peak of 160 mph winds on the 31st. It steadily weakened as it moved westward, and passed by southern Taiwan on September 5th as a minimal typhoon. Wendy continued to weaken, and after crossing the South China Sea, Wendy dissipated over northern Vietnam on the 9th.

~HTTP://WWW.WIKIPEDIA.ORG/, 2010

Early September, 1968—Camp Eagle, South Vietnam

As far as I could see, all low-lying areas were flooded. The ocean extended inland almost to the city of Hue. One fair-sized hill rose above the surrounding water, and apparently, someone decided that the enemy would have gone there to avoid drowning. I stood with a group of pilots as we watched a flight of Hueys, silhouetted against the early-morning sun, make a slow turn toward the hill that was still undergoing an intense artillery barrage. White smoke appeared in the air over the landing zone. The gunships commenced firing on the trees at the top of the hill, and the Hueys landed in a tight formation. It was a flawless combat assault. We all cheered.

"Bercaw, they're waiting for you."

My tour of duty had ended, and I now began my journey home. I thought I should feel something like jubilation; instead, I felt lonely—lonely and guilty. Those who were remaining had jobs to do, and they had already distanced themselves from me. Feeling somewhat like an outcast and nearly overwhelmed with an emotion that I could not comprehend, I picked up my gear, took a look around, said a couple of quick goodbyes, and walked to the waiting Huey.

We had spent the preceding couple of days trying, with limited success, to stay dry in a wind-driven rain that literally came through the sides of the tents.

"Everyone outside. We have to sandbag the helicopters!" I am not certain who yelled this during the first night, but we all scrambled outside into the stinging rain.

"Place as many sandbags as you can find on the skids," yelled Captain Kearns.

I ran down the side of the hill beside our tents where we parked many of the helicopters. Sandbags were scattered randomly around the area in preparation for the construction of additional protective revetments around the Hueys.

"Put them near the front of the skids," someone yelled.

I carried several bags over. Then, just for the hell of it, I removed the cover from the Pitot tube, opened the pilot's door and looked inside at the airspeed indicator. It registered about eighty-two knots (approximately ninety-four miles per hour).

"Man, this is a hell of a storm," someone yelled.

"It's a typhoon," someone else said.

"What's a typhoon?"

"It's what they call hurricanes in this part of the world."

Just that day we had moved our tents to their new locations. Previously, they had covered waist-deep holes that bulldozers had dug into the ground. Now they were on wooden decks and supported by wooden frameworks. Before the typhoon moved past us we would all be ever so happy for this change.

Back in my tent, I did not know what to do, as someone had shut the generators down and it was pitch black inside. We had the flaps of the tents held out with large tent poles, and we decided to leave them in place as the canvas material was doing very little to stop the rain from coming through the sides. I rummaged through my gear using my flashlight and found the khaki uniform that I would wear home, my shoes, and my hat. Along with some underwear, I wrapped them inside my poncho to keep them dry. Everything else was going to get wet.

With nothing else to do, I lay down on my cot. Just as I got reasonably comfortable, something ripped through the side of the tent and landed on my bunk striking my right arm.

"Jesus Christ. What the hell is this?"

All I could think was that a rocket had crashed through the tent and landed on the bunk with me. Certain that it was going to explode at any moment, I jumped up and ran to the end of the tent.

Another pilot came over with a flashlight. The wind had apparently jerked loose one of the big tent poles and flung it into the tent so that it rested on my cot. This brought a round of hoots from everyone.

"A tent pole? Jesus! I'm going home tomorrow. Who wants to be killed by a stupid tent pole?"

The rain drenched us all night, and morning brought no relief. I would not be going home for at least one more day. We had C-Rations for breakfast. I was sick of C-Rations. I ate them only because I was bored, and I had nothing to do but wait out the storm. A newer lieutenant and I found a large sheet of plywood that was just wide and long enough to cover two cots. We pulled our cots together and balanced the wood on poles that we tied to our cots so that we could crawl under the contraption and stay relatively dry. I stayed there almost all day, not willing to venture out into the rain and mud.

That night the rain ended. By morning, the sun shone down on the flooded landscape. I dressed, gathered up the few items that I intended to take with me, and turned in my issued equipment. The armorer rejected my offer to clean my pistol, now covered with rust from the storm. A strong sense of unease accompanied me as I walked out to wait for my ride to Da Nang. No one could see a quick end to the war. I felt guilty about leaving the job unfinished—a job I had believed in and still believed in, if only we would fight to win. This tinged my relief over having survived the year. Nonetheless, I was leaving Vietnam. I did not yet understand that Vietnam would never leave me.

50
90th Replacement Depot

And still, there are things worth fighting for.

~GENERAL H. NORMAN SCHWARZKOPF

September, 1968—Bien Hoa, South Vietnam

One. Two. Three. Four. Five. I counted the mortars leaving their tubes. They were close by.

Whump, whump, whump, whump. And then there was silence. Only four explosions. Was the fifth one heading straight for me?

Squirming around in almost complete darkness, I finally found my cigarettes. I shook one out of the package and placed it in my mouth then looked for a match.

"Fuck."

"What?" a voice asked from behind the glow of a cigarette. He was sitting beside me in the bunker.

"Matches," I said. "I don't have any."

"Here." He handed me his cigarette.

My hands shook, and I had difficulty getting the end of his lit cigarette to the end of mine.

"You must either be very new or you're headed home," the voice said.

"Home in about five hours."

Whump, whump, whump, whump, whump. All five shells exploded this time.

Motherfuckers! It was too late in the game to die. The war, for me, was over. I had done my time and seen enough combat to justify the hazardous-duty pay. I had received my been-there, done-that medals. I had made friends, lost friends, and discovered a lot about myself. Now I just wanted to go somewhere where I would not have to carry a weapon, and I could sleep without worrying about dying before I woke up.

My unknown companion and I sat there in the darkness smoking and saying very little. Finally deciding that it was safe to leave the bunker, we emerged into the predawn light. Too hyped to sleep, I decided to shower and prepare for the trip home.

I looked around and marveled at how the Army had fixed the place up. In addition to nice barracks with cement floors, bunks, and clean sheets, they served great food in the mess hall. Furthermore, the shower offered scalding hot water, a cement floor, and nice wooden benches. It was heaven.

I stood in the shower for a long time, thinking of nothing while relishing the feeling of the sensually hot water running down the length of my body. I tried to position myself so that it encompassed my body completely.

As I stood there enjoying the shower, I watched a frog hopping around the perimeter. Eventually, it began to stir something deep in my mind. I had seen this frog before. I stared at it for a while, trying to remember. Then it hit me. This same frog had taken a shower with Frank and me long ago on our first morning in Vietnam. Realization came slowly. This was the same shower, the same barracks, the same bunks, the same clean sheets, and the same food—just normal military chow. I, on the other hand, had changed. My perceptions were altered after a year of cold showers or no showers, sleeping in the back of the aircraft or on a canvas cot, eating more C-Rations than I could remember, and lugging around a ton of equipment everywhere I went—all while being constantly dog-assed tired. Now, I viewed my surroundings as something close to the lap of luxury.

While dressing, I sorted through the things I was taking home, and I threw much of it, my jungle uniforms, souvenirs, and my dinged and dirty flight helmet, in the garbage. For reasons I have never fully understood, I divested myself of nearly everything that I owned as I prepared to leave Vietnam.

Four hours later, the big DC-8 began its takeoff roll. All talk ceased until it lifted off the runway, and then a loud cheer echoed throughout the plane. I did not cheer. I remained tense until we crossed the coast and headed out over the ocean. Then and only then did I lean back and make an effort to relax. This effort would take years.

Postscript

After landing at Fort Dix, New Jersey, we had to go through a bullshit briefing to which no one paid any attention causing me to miss the last flight out of Philadelphia to Chicago. I spent my first night back in the United States sleeping on a bench in the airport terminal. As I waited for my flight the next morning, I noticed people staring at me, but no one said or did anything. I did not think too much about it. I did not yet understand that public sentiment had turned against the war and many people viewed those who served in a negative context.

Returning to so-called normal life required a bit of a mental adjustment, and it took years to complete. I believed then, and I still believe, that it is a mistake to take men and women out of a combat zone and drop them off at home the next day. There should be some sort of decompression period in which military personnel spend time in the company of others who have shared similar experiences.

People who have not experienced combat simply cannot understand what it is like. No matter how realistic they are, movies and books cannot communicate this experience. People listen politely to our stories and then grow tired of hearing about the war. They expect us to move on, and to some extent, we do. However, nearly forty-five years after I departed Vietnam my memories seem as vivid as if I had returned home no more than a year ago.

For several years, it was difficult for me to take anything seriously. After the most intense period of my life, nothing seemed to be worth the effort. Had I not been married with a child on the way, I am not certain that I would have made the necessary effort to continue my life in a meaningful manner. Joining the Illinois Army National Guard and spending seventeen years there among men with similar experiences was a valuable form of therapy. I highly recommend it.

I am intensely proud of the time I spent as an Army Aviator. There was one bright and shining moment in my professional life; I spent it flying helicopters in Vietnam. I have never regretted it, nor would I exchange the experience for anything this life has to offer. Sometimes, I miss it.

Epilogue

Mission: Failed

Deep into the darkness peering, long I stood there, wondering, fearing.

~EDGAR ALLAN POE

Sitting in the lone helicopter in a large field of yellow grasses, I peer intently at the jungle a couple hundred yards away to the front and perhaps three hundred yards to my left. Straight out from my left door, one hundred yards or less, stands a small grove of trees. I see no one, but I feel very exposed, and I want to leave.

A bullet crashes into the aft portion of the aircraft, back by the tail boom. The sound of it startles me. Anticipating more, I force myself to sit and wait. Another one hits the helicopter, but I cannot determine where. I have no crew. *Where in the hell is everyone?* We need to get out of here.

I scan the edge of the jungle, trying to determine the enemy's location. Nothing. I see nothing in the small grove of trees, but certainly, the firing is coming from there.

Sit and wait—that is all I can do. There is a lot of helicopter they can hit, I tell myself, without hitting me, but then two rounds slam into the panel immediately behind my head causing me to flinch.

I open my eyes and stare into the darkness for a long time, feeling both relief and an underlying sense of failure. I did not complete the mission.

Over the years, I have revisited this field of yellow grasses again and again—always waiting, just waiting.

Huey

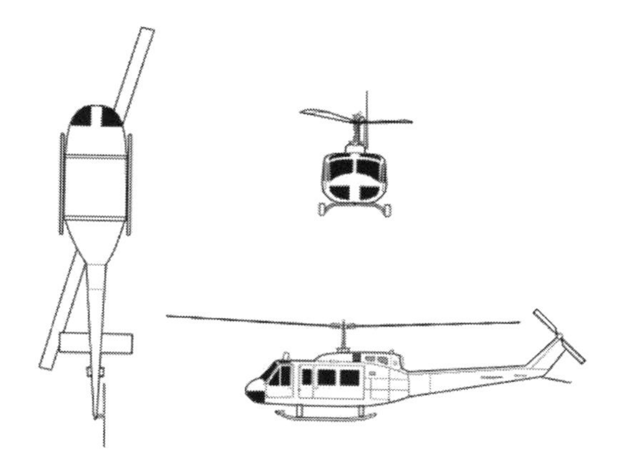

The production of Bell Helicopter's winning entry in the Air Force competition to develop a turbine-engine helicopter began in 1959. It entered the Army inventory as the HU-1 Iroquois. Somehow, this designation became Huey,[25] and it is still the unofficial name for the redesignated UH-1 Iroquois helicopter—the helicopter that is most identified with the Vietnam War.

The first Hueys arrived in Vietnam in 1962. However, it quickly became apparent that the earlier models were not up to the load demands that the heat, humidity, and mountains of Vietnam placed on them. In addition, the earliest versions did not have sufficient cargo space for the types and the sizes of the loads required by an army in action. Numerous model changes followed. The helicopter's progression included the A model, followed quickly by the B

25 The name became so popular that Bell had it cast on the helicopter's anti-torque pedals.

model. The C model had a bigger engine and more robust rotor system. The D model had both a longer fuselage and rotor, which allowed for more passengers and cargo. The E model was for the Marines, and the F model was for the Air Force. The H model was the most-produced version and it had a more powerful engine. The M model came next—essentially, a C model with the more powerful engine used on the H model. The N model was a twin-engine version made for the Air Force, the Navy, and the Marines.

Configured for several different roles, the Huey was a versatile aircraft performing duties such as medevac, gunships, and slicks (troop carrier, resupply and other general missions). In addition, the Huey performed several specialized tasks such as sniffer missions, which involved detecting the scents emanating from groups of humans, such as ammonia from urine. Firefly missions were night interdiction missions using powerful searchlights. Smoke ship missions would spread a thick cloud of smoke between the enemy and friendly troops to obscure the enemy's vision during a combat operation.

The Huey's canvas passenger seats were rarely used in Vietnam, as getting into and out of seats takes time, a commodity that is usually in short supply in a combat environment, and they restrict the type and quantity of payloads. The cargo doors were generally pinned in the open position or removed, due to the heat and because they require time to open and close.

Used by every branch of the U.S. military and by numerous other countries, approximately 7,000 UH-1s served in Vietnam. Combat and accidents claimed nearly half of them.

Once called the Cadillac of helicopters, most crewmembers remember them fondly. The demands of combat required the pilots to fly the UH-1s in circumstances that exceeded anything the designers had considered while it was still on the drawing boards. The Hueys, and all helicopters, flew in harsh environmental conditions of high temperatures, high altitudes, and abrasive dirt and debris. UH-1s were frequently overloaded, and departures sometimes required sliding takeoffs with the cyclic control pulled as far aft as possible to compensate for the skewed center of gravity. The rotor blades would cone upward into a frightening V shape guaranteed to add a couple of beats to each crewmember's pulse rate. The assumption was that the engine would burn off enough fuel before reaching the destination that the center of gravity would shift back to near normal and allow something like a standard landing. Most pilots routinely flew these helicopters with patched bullet holes and at times with fresh combat damage. Collectively, UH-1s flew over seven million hours during the course of the war.

Some Hueys crashed and some sustained crippling combat damage. Adrenalin-fueled pilots banged them into the ground, bent and spread the skids, over-torqued the transmission, stressed the engine, and used the rotor blades as machetes to chop tree limbs as they descended into small jungle clearings to deliver supplies and take out wounded soldiers. And still they flew. I am eternally grateful to Bell Helicopter and their beautiful Huey for bringing me home every time—no matter how badly we had abused her.

Anyone familiar with the Vietnam War knows the sound of a Huey approaching. That crack of the rotor blades beating the air was "the soundtrack of our war."[26] Felt in our breast like a second heart, it was calming. It was exciting. It was powerful. It was frightening. It was love. I, like many, hope that one day I will again hear those pounding blades alerting me that an old friend is coming to take me on one last journey.

---

26 Joe L. Galloway, July 2, 2000, during the Vietnam Helicopter Pilots Association memorial at The Vietnam Veterans Memorial Wall.

John Bercaw, somewhere near the Philippines with the Marines, early 1962

Frank Belsky, summer 1966, prior to reentering the military

Jim Morgan, Song Be, early 1968
Photo courtesy Jim Morgan

Morgan and Rich Neal, Song Be, early 1968
Photo courtesy Jim Morgan

Rubbing from The Vietnam Veterans Memorial Wall in Washington, DC

Bercaw and Belsky, Fort Wolters, Texas, December, 1966

Photo taken by Howard D. Anderson, Class # 67-13, KIA December 27, 1967

Bercaw receiving the Purple Heart Medal from General Barsanti, 101st Airborne Division Commander, Phuoc Vinh, July 4, 1968

Photo courtesy 101st Airborne Division

Crew chief Samsel, gunner Ragland, and Bercaw, mid 1968

Photo courtesy Jim Morgan

Chuck Hagan, Phuoc Vinh, 1968

Photo courtesy of Chuck Hagan

Milo Overstreet, Ben Hoa, early 1968
Photo courtesy of Milo Overstreet

Al Fritz, Camp Eagle, April, 1968
Photo courtesy of Al Fritz

Overstreet, Bercaw, and Fritz heading to town with the bottle of rum, Phuoc Vinh, July, 1968
Photo courtesy Jim Morgan

Following Overstreet north along the coast shortly after the beginning of Tet 1968

Left to right: JJ Mateer, Milo Overstreet, Brian Wold, Herb Klein, Jim Morgan, Al Fritz & Chuck Hagan at Milo's home in Elephant Butte, New Mexico, June, 2011

After-Action Report

- **Frank Belsky** took a direct commission and spent ten years on active duty before joining the Army Reserve and eventually retiring as a Major with twenty-four years of military service. After retiring from private practice law, he spent three years in Afghanistan as a Justice Advisor to the Afghan government in the employ of the State Department's Bureau of International Narcotics and Law Enforcement. Frank and his wife Dee live in Omaha, Nebraska.

- **Jim Morgan** took a direct commission before resigning from the Army after eight years of service. Retired from the Federal Aviation Administration, he and his wife Joan divide their time between Absecon, New Jersey and Greek Peak, New York.

- **Milo Overstree**t is a retired accountant. He and his wife Yvette are living happily in Elephant Butte, New Mexico.

- **Al Fritz** is retired from QuikTrip Corporation, where he was the Director of Real Estate for four of their markets. After retiring, he worked for five years in Farmland Industries' Real Estate Department, and now he and his son own rental units, and buy and flip houses. Al and his wife Rosa live in Lenexa, Kansas.

- **Chuck Hagan** is a lawyer who works and lives in Kentucky.

Internet and Other Information

For additional information about the helicopters, the pilots and the flight crews in Vietnam, visit these Websites:

- Vietnam Helicopter Pilots Association:
  http://www.vhpa.org/
- Vietnam Helicopter Flight Crew Network:
  http://www.vhfcn.org/
- Heli-Vets
  http://www.heli-vets.net/
- Troop D (Air) 1st Sqn 4th U.S. Cavalry:
  http://www.darkhorsevietnam.com/
- A Co., 101st Avn Bn, 101st Airborne Div:
  http://www.a101avn.org/
- USMC/Combat Helicopter Association:
  http://www.popasmoke.com/
- The Combat Helicopter Pilots Association (provides information regarding helicopter pilots in all conflicts):
  http://www.chpa-us.org/

- Additionally, I recommend the following book. Thompson, Neal F., *RECKONING: Vietnam and America's Cold War Experience, 1945-1991*, Naperville, Illinois, Charlevoix Books, 2013, ISBN: 978-0615622729—This is an excellent, controversial book about Vietnam, the political climate leading up to the war, the war itself, and the aftermath of the war. It is available from Amazon.com.

- Readers are welcome to contact the author via john@johnbercaw.com, if they have any questions or comments regarding the people or events in this book.

- Video Links
    - Huey startup and flight. http://www.youtube.com/watch?v=lKCxJpIrkbw
    - Army helicopter flight school, circa 1966. http://www.youtube.com/watch?v=I87f8Q1Ghus
    - Still photos of the helicopter in Vietnam. http://www.youtube.com/watch?v=bg9e4B3pLQA
    - Galloway, Joe. "God's Own Lunatics." http://www.youtube.com/watch?v=F_gJTsRSd38

Glossary

.51-Caliber Machine Gun .... The VC and the NVA sometimes used Chinese 12.7mm/.51-caliber machine guns. These were very effective weapons against troops and helicopters. "See also *VC* and *NVA*"

100-mile-per-hour-tape............ Green duct tape.

Aeroscout .... Smaller helicopters that flew low and slow over the jungle in an attempt to spot the enemy and enemy resources.

Aircraft Attitude .... An aircraft's orientation with respect to the horizon, i.e. nose high or low, and wings level or not.

Altitude .... In aviation, altitude usually refers to height above sea level, but it can also refer to the height above the ground.

Arc Light .... A devastating air attack by B-52 aircraft capable of delivering nearly thirty tons of conventional bombs with great precision. "See also *B-52*"

ARVN .... The Army of the Republic of Vietnam. "See also *Marvin the ARVN*"

Ash-and-Trash Missions......... Sometimes referred to as ass-and-trash, it was slang for resupply missions, moving miscellaneous personnel around the area and other routine missions.

Autorotation .... A descending maneuver in which the engine is disengaged from the main rotor system, and the rotor blades continue turning due solely to the upward flow of air through the rotor system. This maneuver allows for a single landing.

B-52 .... A large Cold-War aircraft originally designed to deliver and drop nuclear weapons on the Soviet Union.

BDA .... Bomb Damage Assessment: a mission to determine the amount of damage inflicted from an attack on the enemy—usually conducted after an Arc Light by B-52s. "See also *B-52* and *Arc Light*"

C and C ship .... Command and Control. This is the aircraft carrying the person in overall command of the mission.

C-130 .... A four-engine turboprop transport aircraft designed and built by Lockheed. Originally designed as an aircraft for troops, medical evacuations, and cargo transportation, it was capable of using unprepared runways for takeoffs and landings.

C-7A .... A smaller twin-engine cargo aircraft that has excellent STOL capabilities. Originally, it was an Army aircraft designated the CV-2. The Air Force took it over in 1962 and redesignated it as the C-7A. "See also *STOL*"

CAR-15 .... A shortened version of the M-16, the rifle most associated with the Vietnam War. The CAR-15 had a collapsible stock and shortened barrel. "See also *M-16*"

Chalk .... Military aircraft in formation refer to themselves by the word *chalk* and their position in the formation. For example, the second aircraft in the formation would be Chalk 2.

Charlie .... Slang for the VC or Viet Cong. Using the military phonetic alphabet, VC is pronounced "Victor Charlie." Over time, this became just "Charlie." "See also *VC* and *Viet Cong*"

Check Ride .... A flight the student must take and successfully pass to demonstrate competency in the required skills before proceeding to the next level of instruction.

Chicken Plate .... A curved ceramic plate worn over the chest. It is capable of stopping .30-caliber armor-piercing ammunition.

Chinook.................................... A twin-engine, tandem rotor, heavy-lift helicopter.

Claymore Mine .... A command-detonated, directional, anti-personnel mine that fires steel balls out into a fan-shaped kill zone.

Click .... Military maps are metric and each grid square, called a click (also spelled "klick"), is equal to one kilometer on the ground. It is equivalent to .62 miles.

CO .... Commanding Officer.

Cobra .... Built by Bell Helicopter, it was the first successful helicopter built strictly for an attack role. Designated the AH-1, it featured a streamlined, narrow-width fuselage that carried a two-man crew in tandem seats with the pilot above and behind the co-pilot/gunner.

Collective .... The collective pitch control changes the pitch angle of all the main rotor blades at the same time, thereby increasing or decreasing the total lift provided by the rotor system.

Concertina Wire........................ a type of barbed wire or razor wire formed in large coils that expand like a concertina. The military uses it to create obstacles.

Cover.. The military term for a hat or cap.

Cyclic .... The cyclic control changes the angle of the rotor blades, causing the rotor disk to tilt in a particular direction. As a result, the helicopter moves in that direction.

C-Rations .... Meal Combat Individual, called C-Rations, was an individual meal contained in cans and foil packets. Infantry and other units who were out of range of traditional prepared meals commonly used it.

DC-8 .... Large commercial aircraft used extensively to ferry military personnel to and from Vietnam.

Dead Man's Zone .... The altitudes between fifty feet and 1,500 feet. Below fifty feet, the exposure time when an enemy could successfully target an aircraft was limited and 1,500 feet was above the effective range of most weapons available to the average enemy soldier.

Deck .... The term for floor in the Navy and Marines.

Deuce and a half...................... 2.5 ton truck.

Dink .... A disparaging term for a North Vietnamese soldier or guerrilla in the Vietnam War. "See also *Gook*"

Distinguished Flying Cross ... A medal awarded to anyone who "distinguished himself by heroism or extraordinary achievement while participating in aerial flight." It is not restricted to combat heroism.

DMZ .... Demilitarized Zone: an area between two or more military powers where military action is forbidden. The U.S. military honored the DMZ between North and South Vietnam, but the North Vietnamese ignored the status of the area. This gave them a safe haven from which to launch attacks into South Vietnam.

Donut Dolly .... Female Red Cross worker.

Dustoff .... Dustoff was the call sign assigned to most U.S. Army medical evacuation helicopter units in South Vietnam. The exception was the 1st Cavalry Division, which used the call sign Medevac.

Fast Mover .... A term Army helicopter pilots used for Air Force jets because they were so much faster than the helicopters.

Fatigues .... Army work uniform.

Flechette Rounds .... Nasty antipersonnel artillery rounds containing approximately 10,000 small-finned steel darts that spread in a very effective and extremely devastating pattern. The troops called them beehive rounds because of the buzzing sound that they made as they streaked toward a target.

FM Homing Device .... A device used for determining the general direction to a location based on radio signals from that location.

FM Radio .... Radios used for communications by smaller military units working in a tactical environment.

FNG .... Fucking New Guy: a disparaging term for men just arriving in Vietnam.

Friendly Fire............................ Misdirected gunfire or artillery fire coming from your own or your allies' forces.

GCA .... Ground Controlled Radar Approach for aircraft.

Go-around................................ An aborted landing of an aircraft that is on final approach.

Gook .... A highly offensive term for somebody of East Asian or Southeast Asian descent. "See also *Dink*"

Gunship .... A helicopter configured specifically as an attack helicopter.

Hatch... A term for doorway in the Navy and Marines.

High-Overhead Approach...... This procedure allows a helicopter to fly to its destination from the safety of altitude. Once over the landing zone the pilot descends over relatively safe territory while keeping the exposure time at the lower altitudes to a minimum. Crossing over the destination in the direction of the intended landing the pilot begins a turning descent while reducing airspeed. At the completion of a 360° turn, the aircraft should be touching down.

Hootch .... Slang for a place to live, or a shelter that is usually temporary in nature.

Hootch Maid .... a South Vietnamese woman employed to clean the hootch, do laundry, and polish boots, etc. for American servicemen. "See also *Hootch*"

HQ .... Abbreviation for headquarters.

JP-4 .... Fuel designed for use in aircraft powered by gas-turbine engines.

Jungle Fatigues .... The working uniform used by most U.S. military personnel in Vietnam.

KIA .... Killed in Action.

Knot .... One nautical mile: 6,076 feet, a unit of length equivalent to 1.852 kilometers and 1.151 miles. 100 knots per hour is equal to approximately 115 miles per hour.

Laterite....................................... Soil rich in iron oxide. It forms in regions where the climate is warm and humid, and it is blackish brown to reddish in color.

LZ .... Landing Zone.

M1 .... A semi-automatic rifle first used in WWII. It had limited duty in the early stages of the Vietnam War. "See also *M-14* and *M-16*"

M-14 .... Based on the M1 rifle. It saw limited service early in the Vietnam War before the M-16 became the standard issue weapon. It is the basis for some of today's sniper rifles. "See also *M1* and *M-16*"

M-16 .... The rifle used by most U.S. and allied forces during the Vietnam War. "See also *CAR-15, M1* and *M-14*"

M-60 .... The standard machine-gun that the infantry and other units used. Most Huey helicopters had one mounted in each door to provide the crew with immediate and temporary suppressive fire.

Marvin the Arvin..................... ARVN (Army of the Republic of Vietnam) was pronounced "Arvin" by U.S. troops. As a result, Americans called South Vietnamese soldiers "Marvin the Arvin." "See also *ARVN*"

Mini-gun .... A six-barreled machine gun that is capable of firing 4,000 to 6,000 rounds per minute.

Montagnard (*mon-tuhn-yahrd*) French for "mountain dweller," this refers to indigenous people inhabiting the mountains and highlands of southern Vietnam.

NVA .... North Vietnamese Army.

OH-13... A Korean War-era helicopter used for observation early in the Vietnam War. The S model saw the most use in Vietnam.

One-Over-the-World Map...... 1:250,000 scale map. Most infantry and helicopter pilots used 1:50,000 or 1:25,000 scale maps.

P-38 .... A rectangular piece of stamped metal, used for opening C-Ration cans. Grooved down the center for extra strength, it was just big enough to grasp firmly between the thumb and the forefinger.

Parachute Landing Fall .... (PLF) A technique that allows a parachutist to land safely without being injured.

Passageway.............................. A term for hallway in the Navy and Marines.

Pedal Turn .... Anything observed while looking down through the thick jungle could be lost and never found again if not kept constantly in sight. When spotting a target the OH-13 scout pilots would press full left pedal, thus causing the helicopter to make a very tight turn. This allowed the pilot to keep the object in sight.

Perfume River.......................... This river flows through Hue, the old imperial capital of Vietnam.

Pitot (*pee-toe*) **Tube**.................... A pressure-sensitive instrument used to determine the airspeed of an aircraft.

Platoon...................................... For the purposes of this book, a platoon is the smallest cohesive military unit.

Preflight .... A procedure for checking an aircraft for airworthiness before flight.

Prog or Progress Ride .... The first step in eliminating a student pilot from further flight training.

Pucker Factor............................. A term, referring to the tightness of the sphincter muscle, used to describe the stress level just before or during a dangerous situation.

Purple Heart .... A medal awarded for wounds received in armed conflict with an enemy of the United States. The wound must have required treatment by a medical officer.

Push .... Assigned radio frequency.

PX .... Post Exchange: a military general store.

PZ .... Pickup Zone.

Quonset Hut.............................. A lightweight structure of corrugated galvanized steel that has a semicircular cross-section.

REMF.. Rear Echelon Motherfucker. Pronounced exactly as spelled, it is a derogatory term for military personnel stationed in relatively safe rear areas.

Revetment.................................. In Vietnam, a structure designed to protect aircraft against damage from explosives.

RPG .... Rocket-Propelled Grenade.

RPM .... Revolutions Per Minute.

Run Up .... The process of starting the helicopter.

S-3 (Air) .... The person responsible for all aviation activities in their operational area.

Semper Fidelis .... *Always Faithful.* This is the United States Marine Corps motto, frequently pronounced "Semper Fi."

Short-Timer Calendar .... In Vietnam it was a device (frequently a drawing of a nude woman divided into 365 sections, sort of like a Paint By Numbers picture) used by soldiers to count their remaining days in the country.

Skid .... The landing gear for a Huey that consists of two aluminum tubes, reinforced with steel skid shoes attached to the bottom to minimize wear, connected by two arched cross tubes.

Slick .... A Huey helicopter not rigged as a gunship was called a slick because it did not have guns and rockets hanging off the sides or under the nose.

Smoke .... The Army in Vietnam extensively used grenades that emitted smoke of differing colors to identify locations otherwise difficult for pilots to find in the pervasive jungle.

Split-S Maneuver .... Used by fighter pilots to disengage from combat, the pilot half-rolls his airplane inverted and makes a descending half-loop. This results in level flight in the opposite direction at a lower altitude.

Stage Field .... A small airfield designed for training Army flight students.

STOL .... Short Take Off and Landing. This was a desirable trait for aircraft operating in an environment with short or non-existent runways.

TAC Officer .... Training, Advising, and Counseling Officer assigned to each training group "to train and identify, in a select group of soldiers, the necessary traits of leadership, mental and physical abilities, and moral values that will qualify them to become future

Warrant Officers." United States Army Combined Arms Center, Accessed April 9, 2013, http://usacac.army.mil/cac2/WOCC/repository/WOCS_TAC_Officers.pdf

TET .... Vietnamese Lunar New Year.

TH-13T.. An OH-13 helicopter modified as an instrument-training aircraft for the U.S. Army.

TOC .... Tactical Operations Center. It was the headquarters for units in the field.

Translational Lift .... The extra lift generated as the helicopter passes through about 16–20 knots of airspeed. This is the result of the rotor system passing into clean air or air that has not been disturbed while the helicopter speed is slow or while hovering.

UH-1B Huey .... An older, smaller Huey used early in the war. It had insufficient power for the demands placed on it.

UH-1H Huey .... the most-produced version had a longer fuselage and a more powerful engine.

UHF Radio .... An Ultra-High-Frequency radio with a range between 300 MHz and 33,000 MHz.

Utilities.. Marine Corps work uniform.

VHF Radio .... A Very-High-Frequency radio with a range between 30 MHZ to 300 MHz.

Viet Cong....................................... The guerrilla force that fought against South Vietnam and the United States and its allies with the support of the North Vietnamese Army. "See also *VC* and *Charlie*"

VC .... Viet Cong. "See also *Viet Cong* and *Charlie*"

WORWAC .... Warrant Officer Rotary Wing Aviation Course. An intensive nine-month army training program designed to teach students to become officers and helicopter pilots.

XO .... Executive Officer.

Biography

After four years in the Marine Corps, John Bercaw joined the United States Army and spent a year in Vietnam as a helicopter pilot. After Vietnam, he served as an instrument instructor pilot at Hunter Army Airfield in Georgia before joining the Illinois Army National Guard where he remained until 1990, retiring as a Chief Warrant Officer 4 and a Master Army Aviator. His medals include the Distinguished Flying Cross, Bronze Star with oak leaf cluster, Purple Heart, Meritorious Service Medal, Air Medal with the "V" device and the numeral 21, Marine Corps Good Conduct Medal, Vietnam Service Medal with four campaign stars, Vietnam Gallantry Cross Medal with Bronze Star, and Republic of Vietnam Campaign Medal. He earned a B.A. from Aurora University, Aurora, Illinois in 1977 and worked for the Federal Government. Upon retirement, he spent nine years as an instructor at Waubonsee Community College in Illinois, and now lives with his wife Cynthia in Kentucky.

Made in the USA
Charleston, SC
10 November 2013